DETROIT'S
SOJOURNER TRUTH
HOUSING RIOT OF 1942

DETROIT'S
SOJOURNER TRUTH
HOUSING RIOT OF 1942

PRELUDE TO THE RACE RIOT OF 1943

GERALD VAN DUSEN

THE
History
PRESS

Published by The History Press
Charleston, SC
www.historypress.com

Copyright © 2020 by Gerald Van Dusen
All rights reserved

First published 2020

ISBN 9781540243942

Library of Congress Control Number: 2020938460

CONTENTS

FOREWORD

Professor Van Dusen is a friend and partner of the Fair Housing Center of Metropolitan Detroit in our mission to achieve equal housing opportunities for all. *Detroit's Sojourner Truth Housing Riot of 1942* graphically illustrates the importance of equal housing opportunities.

I have lived in the metropolitan Detroit area for over sixty years and lived in three homes in the city of Detroit and in homes in the immediate suburbs. I thought I knew about Detroit's Birwood Wall, commonly known as the "8 Mile Wall." The wall was built in 1941 to racially separate a white neighborhood from a black neighborhood, illustrating metropolitan Detroit's sad and tragic history of racial division and segregation. The fact that the wall was constructed to assist white residents in obtaining federally funded financing shows governmental complicity and involvement in racist housing practices.

That is, I thought I had a good understanding of the Birwood Wall—and the metropolitan Detroit area—until I read Professor Van Dusen's widely acclaimed book *Detroit's Birwood Wall: Hatred and Healing in the West Eight Mile Community*. In *Detroit's Birwood Wall*, Professor Van Dusen puts the Birwood Wall in its historical context. The wall was built after decades of segregation and oppression of black residents of Detroit, as well as an even larger population of black immigrants from the South, in terms of housing, education, public accommodations, transportation, healthcare and other areas of everyday life. *Detroit's Birwood Wall* provided a clear, chronological picture of what had been scattered historical events.

After reading *Detroit's Birwood Wall*, I was stunned by the decades of exclusion and subjugating segregation of black Detroit residents and large numbers of black immigrants. I could now look at Detroit and the surrounding suburbs and understand why the metropolitan Detroit area remains so highly segregated. I was also disappointed that no one ever had explained metropolitan Detroit's racial background in a clear fashion.

Professor Van Dusen does the same thing in *Detroit's Sojourner Truth Housing Riot of 1942*. He places the Sojourner Truth Housing Riot of 1942 in a clear, chronological context. Reading *Detroit's Sojourner Truth Housing Riot of 1942* is like watching events in a movie unfold. As Professor Van Dusen puts it: "The trouble began, it can be said, with a single letter." Viewing the buildup of racial rhetoric and hostility leading up to the letter and the following chain of events resulting in the race riot, one is left to question how residents and community leaders, as well as local, state and federal government officials, will deal with racially charged events in the future.

I appreciate two aspects of Professor Van Dusen's writing. First, it is apparent that Professor Van Dusen is not writing to convince his readers. *Detroit's Sojourner Truth Housing Riot of 1942*, like *Detroit's Birwood Wall*, is meticulously researched. He offers little commentary and allows the facts to speak for themselves. *Detroit's Sojourner Truth Housing Riot of 1942* shows the failure of leadership at all levels.

Second, Professor Van Dusen, as an English professor, is a gifted writer. *Detroit's Sojourner Truth Housing Riot of 1942*, like *Detroit's Birwood Wall*, is exceptionally well written. Those with busy schedules will appreciate Professor Van Dusen's effective communication.

There are a couple of things I would like to see. I would like to see *Detroit's Sojourner Truth Housing Riot of 1942* used in high school and college courses. With the aid of a study guide with discussion questions, students should have the opportunity to read and discuss each chapter of the book. It is helpful to know history. It is far more valuable to learn from it.

The questions Professor Van Dusen raises in *Detroit's Sojourner Truth Housing Riot of 1942* naturally lead to discussions. Could one of the worst race riots in American history have been averted? What is it about the political realities of that era that made desegregation not a realistic option? Would more public housing have mitigated some of the racial tension? And how could the largely implacable attitudes and behaviors of white residents and immigrants in interacting with black residents and immigrants in major employment centers, on the streetcars and in

FOREWORD

the public parks and elsewhere have been addressed to achieve racial harmony? These were penetrating questions in that day. They remain penetrating questions in our day.

I WOULD ALSO LIKE to see Professor Van Dusen continue writing on these topics. Perhaps his next books will address the 1943 Detroit race riot, the 12th Street Riot of 1967, the Packard Hate Strike or other events. Professor Van Dusen mentions the 1943 race riot in chapter 2 and in his conclusion. There is little question that Professor Van Dusen would address the 1943 and 1967 riots as well as he has covered Detroit's Sojourner Truth Housing Riot of 1942 in this book and the Birwood Wall in his previous book.

Finally, I would like to see *Detroit's Sojourner Truth Housing Riot of 1942* and Professor Van Dusen's other books reach a nationwide audience. In chapter 5, Professor Van Dusen shows how the Sojourner Truth Housing Riot of 1942 became a national and international issue. The incidents also led to grand jury indictments, though the largely negligible results from the prosecutions would hardly deter subsequent racially motivated criminality. Professor Van Dusen makes sure we learn from this history.

—Steve Tomkowiak
Executive Director
Fair Housing Center of Metropolitan Detroit

INTRODUCTION

On April 29, 1942, just five short months after the infamous attack on Pearl Harbor and President Franklin Delano Roosevelt's impassioned request of Congress for a declaration of war against Japan, Detroiter Walter Jackson, a short, wiry, thirty-five-year-old former UAW-CIO shop steward, prepared for the battle of his life. "We are here now, and let the bad luck happen," Jackson told an on-scene reporter. "I have only got one time to die and I'd just as soon die here."[1]

Jackson was not talking about confronting the Germans on the battlefields of Europe or the Japanese on the islands of the South Pacific. The "enemy" he was about to confront was a large group of fellow Americans—white Americans—hellbent on preventing him, his family and other African American defense workers from moving into a defense housing project on the northeast side of Detroit.

Just six weeks earlier, violence had erupted at the housing project as two hundred black families were forcibly prevented from their scheduled move-in by a large mob of pickets, protesters and outside agitators, whereupon forty individuals were sent to local hospitals and more than two hundred others were arrested and jailed.

The story of the Sojourner Truth Housing Riot of 1942 is a wartime story fought on the homefront, on the streets of Detroit, the true "Arsenal of Democracy." The incident occurred at a time when the White House and officials from various federal agencies were preaching racial unity to counter Nazi claims of Aryan superiority.

INTRODUCTION

Initially described in the media as a "neighborhood squabble," the controversy accelerated quickly to become a citywide political scandal whose resolution would eventually land in the lap of federal officials, where the problem had originated. The controversy would reveal the extent to which the federal government was complicit in segregating urban America and expose the degree to which much of Detroit's politics, its policies and its programs were influenced by internal factionalism.

A CITY OF FACTIONS

At the outbreak of World War II, Detroit was an industrial city of 1.7 million residents. Nearly half of its population had arrived in the previous two decades and were less likely to identify with the city than they were with a religious community, cultural organization or labor union.

Polish Catholics represented the largest single bloc, with over 250,000 residents, not counting the Polish enclave of Hamtramck, a city within Detroit with approximately 50,000 Polish residents. The Polish were typically devout Catholics, filling the pews of thirty-five Polish neighborhood churches.

Approximately 200,000 Southern whites constituted the second-largest group of Detroiters, bringing with them their own indigenous Southern attitudes toward race and religion.

More than 100,000 African Americans settled in Detroit during the first wave of the Great Migration. In 1940, there were 149,000 black residents of the city, and by the end of the 1940s, that number would more than double.

The rest of Detroit's population was made up of long-established ethnic whites (Germans, Italians, Yugoslavs, Bulgarians, Syrians, Irish and others), eastern European Jews, established African Americans and Canadians.

The best illustration of how these various factions interplayed would be in the auto plants, now converted to war production, where unions representing workers targeted management for improved wages and working conditions but internally struggled with members having various agendas: ethnic Catholics who formed as much as 50 percent of union membership and who were seeking to flee poverty yet preserve their ethnic heritage, the communists with their socialistic agenda and goal of workers' control over industry, the African Americans who were seeking redress over constant abuse and employment discrimination, the National Workers League and elements of the Ku Klux Klan who were attempting to sow division among the union rank-and-file and exclude what they perceived as undesirables.

12

BOOMTOWN OR BUST

Detroit in the 1920s and '30s was a city of economic feast or famine. The 1920s saw the city become wealthy from the mass production and sale of automobiles by forty-three different auto manufacturing companies. To accommodate its burgeoning workforce, the city accelerated its program of annexing land in all directions, increasing its size in one ten-year period (1916–26) by 70 square miles, or one-half its size. In 1926, the city was forced to end this program owing to state legislative action and by surrounding communities incorporating as cities to avoid being absorbed by Detroit. The city now occupied 139 square miles but continued to grow its population each year as tens of thousands of Southern migrants flooded into the city in search of factory employment.

By the end of the 1920s and for much of the next decade, Detroit struggled to stay on its feet as the Great Depression took hold. Guardian and First National, Detroit's two largest banks, were liquidated. Auto sales declined by 75 percent. Tens of thousands of residents were thrown out of work. Many families owed their survival to federal programs such as the Civilian Conservation Corps, with its sixty-one camps in Michigan employing over ten thousand young men. By the end of the 1930s, Hitler had annexed Austria and invaded Czechoslovakia. After Germany invaded Poland on September 1, 1939, France and Great Britain declared war. Despite initial declarations of neutrality, the United States would soon be plunged into the Second World War.

EMPLOYMENT GROWTH

Roosevelt and other administration officials knew that complete recovery from the Great Depression would not come about by engaging in another major war. National economic recovery from the Great Depression was far from complete, for double-digit unemployment lingered throughout the 1930s, and by 1939, it hovered around 17 percent. Full participation in any war effort would merely temporarily trade improved employment numbers for a substantial increase in the national debt. (Time would prove Roosevelt's prescience, as nearly 17 million unemployed found work in the various war industries, but the national debt spiraled from $49 billion in 1941 to $260 billion in 1945.) In other words, there was no illusion, from a strictly economic perspective, that World War II would pull the country out of Depression. More importantly, especially following the domestic suffering endured during the Great Depression, few families wanted to send their boys across the ocean to a faraway war.

After France fell to Germany within six weeks during the summer of 1940, Great Britain now stood alone as the only major power confronting the Nazi menace. Roosevelt believed the war would soon be at our doorstep and we needed to be prepared for that eventuality. National polling began to reflect American fears that we would of necessity be drawn into the war, yet we were not fully prepared to commit to any more than helping Great Britain in their darkest hour.

"We must be the great arsenal of democracy," FDR stated on December 29, 1940. "For us this is an emergency as serious as war itself. We must apply ourselves to our task with the same resolution, the same sense of urgency, the same spirit of patriotism and sacrifice as we would show were we at war."

FDR would go on to call for the mass production of guns, ships, tanks and other war materiel to support Great Britain as part of a lend-lease

Sitting at his desk in the Oval Office, President Franklin Delano Roosevelt prepares to deliver an address to the nation. *Library of Congress.*

program. Hermann Goering, one of the primary architects of the Nazi police state, scoffed at such a claim; America was, in his estimation, capable of manufacturing only refrigerators and razor blades. United Auto Workers president Walter Reuther countered by saying, "England's battles, it used to be said, were won on the playing fields of Eton. America's can be won on the assembly lines of Detroit."[2] If FDR could envision *what* needed to be done, Reuther knew *how* it would be done.

FDR knew he would need industrial innovators to fulfill his promise to the American people that the country would be prepared when the time came. Based on the recommendation of longtime adviser Bernard Baruch, FDR asked Detroit's General Motors president William Knutsen to come to Washington to head up the Office of Production Management. His expertise in management and mass production was exactly what would be needed in order to outpace the enemy in the production of military hardware. (After the war, Knutsen could say, "We won because we smothered the enemy in an avalanche of production, the likes of which he had never seen nor dreamed possible.")

Sixteen million Americans joined various branches of the armed forces. Minority participation was significant. All citizens, regardless of racial or ethnic origin, were equally subject to the draft and enjoyed the same rate of pay. Among the minorities in uniform were Chinese, Japanese, Filipinos, Puerto Ricans, Hawaiians and Native Americans. African Americans were an especially important source of manpower for the American military, as two and a half million registered for the draft and over one million were inducted through Selective Service by December 31, 1945. Black inductees constituted approximately 11 percent of all registrants liable for service.

Another twenty-four million Americans worked in factories on the homefront to supply these troops overseas. Cities big and small across the nation responded by transforming themselves almost overnight into centers of armaments production. Shipyards in Boston, Richmond, Mobile and San Diego turned out so much tonnage that by 1943 they had replaced all Allied ships sunk since the beginning of the war in 1939.

As the war raged on, Detroit became the embodiment of FDR's "Arsenal of Democracy." The city constituted 2 percent of the nation's population, yet it accounted for 10 percent of the nation's war materiel output. Having begun the retooling as early as February 1941, Detroit's auto companies were in high gear by the time the country formally entered the war. Detroit assembly lines would produce tanks, amphibious "duck" trucks, airplanes,

William S. Knutsen, former president of General Motors, sifts through notes as he prepares to speak before a congressional subcommittee in his capacity as chairman of the Office of Production Management. *Library of Congress.*

radar units, bombsights, fighter plane engines, aircraft propellers, marine engines and many millions of bullets. Cadillac converted from automobile to tank production in fifty-five days. FDR had vowed the country would produce 60,000 planes by the end of 1942. Ford promised and delivered one 56,000-pound B-24 Liberator (capable of flying 300-plus miles per hour) every hour. By the end of the war, Willow Run had produced 4,600 units of what would become the world's most-produced multiengine heavy bomber in military history.[3]

Once again, Detroit became boomtown. In the first six months after Pearl Harbor, Detroit made $1.4 billion in war materiel, likely more than it would have made in automobile manufacturing during the same period in peacetime. By 1943, the city was expected to produce $12 billion in war goods, according to estimates by the Office of Production Management.

Jobs were plentiful, and wages were good. Given the shortage of young white males in the workforce, newly available positions on the factory floor

Black servicemen examining a grounded fighter plane in Germany. *Library of Congress.*

Factory worker at Briggs Manufacturing, Detroit, Michigan. *Library of Congress.*

Factory worker at Briggs
Manufacturing, Detroit,
Michigan. *Library of Congress.*

were gradually filled by white women and minorities, particularly black men and women. These new employment opportunities and this newfound economic stability encouraged many African Americans to believe they might now be integrated into society and enjoy the same economic mobility enjoyed by the people they replaced. By 1940, nearly 12 percent of Ford line workers were black. However, because of factionalism, workplace tensions escalated between groups, and none suffered the sting of abuse and discrimination more than African Americans.

RACIAL SEGREGATION IN DETROIT

In 1940, no city in the United States was more racially segregated than Detroit, and even today, the Detroit metropolitan area remains deeply segregated. To understand this phenomenon, one must revisit real estate transactions conducted in the United States at the turn of the twentieth century. "Covenants," that is, binding agreements between buyer and seller, are normal elements to be found within the language of property transactions.

Restrictive covenants, too, are often embedded in the language of the deed to the property and "restrict" what property owners can and cannot do with the purchased property. For example, to buy into a new suburban subdivision, the purchaser might be required to honor a homeowners' association requirement that no fences be constructed between individual properties, thus creating an aesthetically pleasing green belt in the backyards of property owners. Racially restrictive covenants, however, began to appear sporadically during the final decade of the nineteenth century, first in Massachusetts and California. The covenant bound the new homeowner to restrict any future sale in such a way as to exclude, for example, African Americans from purchasing the land, perhaps for a specific period or, perhaps, into perpetuity. Such a covenant might read as follows: "Hereafter no part of said property or any portion thereof shall be occupied by any person not of the Caucasian race, it being intended hereby to restrict the use of said property against occupancy as owners or tenants of any portion of said property for resident or other purposes by people of the Negro or Mongolian race."[4]

The Great Migration of blacks from the South beginning around 1910 deeply concerned white property owners nationwide who were averse to any form of integration. Baltimore mayor Barry Mahool summed up the prevailing attitude by suggesting, "Blacks should be quarantined in isolated slums in order to reduce the incidents of civil disturbance, to prevent the spread of communicable disease into the nearby White neighborhoods, and to protect property values among the White majority."[5] While the Supreme Court (in *Buchanan v. Warley*) ruled "racial zoning" within municipalities unconstitutional in 1917, it left open private agreements, such as restrictive covenants. Thus, within a few years, with the organizational support of the real estate industry, racially restrictive covenants proliferated within deeds of sale, not only when property exchanged hands between one buyer and one seller but also within large-scale real estate developments. One estimate suggests that at least 50 percent of all residential property deeds in the United States had racially restrictive covenants by 1948, when the Supreme Court ruled (in *Shelly v. Kramer*) that such covenants were "unenforceable." The damage had been done, but now the problem was finally resolved. Or so it seemed.

In Detroit, like Chicago and many other big cities, it has been estimated that outside the inner city, 80 percent of residential property deeds contained racially restrictive covenants. Before 1948, this left very few areas for blacks to rent or purchase property. Compounding the housing problem created by these restrictions, the African American population more than doubled between 1940 and 1950 (from 149,119 in 1940 to 300,506 in 1950). In 1940, blacks represented 9.19 percent of the city's population. However, ten years later, the effect of the Great Migration could be felt dramatically as blacks now constituted 16.25 percent of the population—and they were a constituency that would increase significantly in both number and percentage in the years ahead.

If housing was a serious problem for Southern whites arriving by the thousands each month before, during and after the war, it was an absolute crisis for black migrants. Several factors were in play. First, when black migrants arrived at the city limits, they were given few immediate housing options. Most had limited financial resources, typically not enough to purchase a home. However, regardless of their financial condition, there were only six areas of the city receptive to black renters or homeowners not subject to the conditions of racially restrictive covenants: Black Bottom, Paradise Valley, North End, Westside, Conant Gardens and Eight Mile–Wyoming. Furthermore, these areas were not socioeconomically equal. Conant Gardens and Westside were two established middle-class black communities with a high percentage of property owners. Here you could find civil servants, teachers, accountants and so on. For economically disadvantaged black migrants arriving from the South, housing options were thus further restricted, and most found themselves settling into the overcrowded and dilapidated rental units found within Black Bottom and Paradise Valley. Despite these squalid conditions, blacks had few other choices and also had to bear the brunt of unscrupulous landlords who knew the demand was so great they could ignore requests for desperately needed repairs to these flats and apartments and still charge exorbitant rent.

While racially restrictive covenants were mainly responsible for racial segregation in the big industrial centers such as Detroit, the effects were further exacerbated by policies and programs that were created before World War II. Following the election of FDR in 1932, a series of New Deal programs and projects were created in response to the dire economic conditions precipitated by the Great Depression. Among the many agencies created were the Federal Housing Administration (FHA) and the Home Loan Bank Board. The FHA was designed to stabilize the housing market by providing insurance on loans tendered by the banking and loan industry. Similarly, under the supervision of the Federal Home Loan Bank Board, the Home Owners' Loan Corporation (HOLC) was authorized to provide new mortgages on an emergency basis to homeowners at risk of losing their homes due to foreclosure.

In 1935, HOLC began deviating from its original mission to assist homeowners avoid losing their homes to foreclosure and, for the next five years, developed a City Survey Program designed to assess risk levels for long-term real estate investment and to stabilize the appraising industry. HOLC agents traveled the country to gather data from local realtors and appraisers in more than two hundred cities. Particular neighborhoods within a city such as Detroit were graded thusly: A, Green, Best; B, Blue, Still Desirable; C, Yellow, Declining; and D, Red, Hazardous. Although the term *redlining* was not coined until the 1960s, it clearly applied in 1940 to neighborhoods with minority occupants, which were considered high risk for mortgage lenders.[6]

For blacks without significant resources, substandard housing and living conditions became a self-fulfilling prophesy. The Eight Mile–Wyoming neighborhood was a case in point. Prospective black homeowners had tried for years to obtain bank financing to construct standard housing. Because banks were unable to secure FHA backing, owing to the hazardous designation determined by HOLC, loan applications from African American settlers in the area were rejected wholesale. And since banks charged private contractors who were willing to build in the area higher interest rates, few residents were able to afford these professional services. Instead, many residents built walls of whatever malleable materials they could find. And still others constructed shacks, piece by piece, as lumber was purchased and scrap material became available locally.

In 1941, a real estate developer had approached the FHA with plans to develop the property west of the black Eight Mile–Wyoming enclave for an exclusively white clientele, only to have his application for federal insurance on loans rejected because the proposed project bordered this hazardous neighborhood, as defined by HOLC's City Survey Program. The FHA was reluctant to insure bank loans on such properties because racially mixed areas, the agency reasoned, were likely to stir confrontation, lead to violence and jeopardize the fiscal soundness of the investment. Undaunted, the developer approached the FHA a second time with a new proposal: he would construct a wall, six feet high and one foot thick, between the hazardous neighborhood east of the wall and the proposed new development. The FHA agreed to the compromise.

Over the years, efforts to further isolate the community, under the guise of protecting property values, would surface. For example, in 1953, Jewish real estate developer Harry Slatkin proposed extending the wall just south of the African American community in a direction perpendicular to the existing wall to further separate the African American community from his Jewish clientele, who were moving in a northerly direction. He would promote the development as "one of northwest Detroit's last and most fashionable residential areas." When the city building department rejected his permit request, he was undeterred. A six-foot-high solid wood fence, six blocks in length, was erected. Eventually, Slatkin's fence deteriorated to the point that it had to be removed. The concrete segregation wall, however, stands to this day.

SUBSTANDARD CONDITIONS IN THE SEGREGATED NEIGHBORHOODS

As Southerners migrated to Detroit, housing became the most critical issue for white and black workers. By 1942, 98.7 percent of all dwelling units in Detroit were occupied (85 percent was considered the housing danger mark). One often had to travel fifty miles to find decent housing to rent. The housing situation was particularly critical for African Americans in this highly segregated industrial center. With the second wave of the Great Migration taking place, housing was in such short supply that people doubled up and lived in cramped quarters, in garages, in carriage houses, in attics, in tents and too often on the street. An average of 10,000 job seekers entered Detroit each month during the early war years. By 1943, Detroit's population had increased by more than 400,000 as a direct consequence of the Great Migration from the South. There was no more land to be annexed and fewer and fewer places to construct housing.

Not only was housing in short supply, but it also was frequently substandard. In 1940, the U.S. Census Bureau undertook to measure for the very first time the nature, extent and condition of the country's housing stock. It found that 45.7 percent of houses in the United States were considered substandard, which was defined at the time as housing that lacked complete plumbing facilities or was dilapidated. Poor housing conditions were thus a nationwide problem, but conditions in black neighborhoods, such as on the lower east side of Detroit, were particularly acute. Most structures in the residential areas were built in the nineteenth

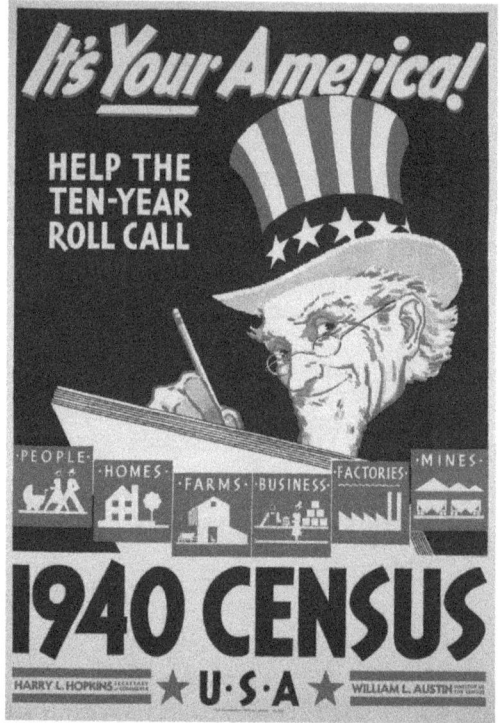

Right: Poster promoting public participation in the 1940 census, the very first to assess the condition of American housing. *Library of Congress.*

Below: Living room in substandard apartment building after sustaining fire damage. Note the coal-burning stove in the middle of the room. *Library of Congress.*

century; however, the problem was not the age of the structure. It was the degree of neglect by unscrupulous landlords who felt no compunction to remedy defects when the demand for accommodations—almost any kind of accommodations—was so great.

From today's perspective, a much clearer picture of substandard housing brings into focus the conditions many African Americans suffered in their quest for safe, clean, affordable housing during the war years. To meet any reasonable living standard, a dwelling should provide access to basic needs: a clean, dry place that reduces exposure to harsh weather, physical injury and communicable diseases and infections; a safe place with functioning utilities such as water, sewer, gas and electricity; and a secure place to rest and relax, as well as to store food, clothing, medications and items of personal hygiene. Few homes in the largest black neighborhoods met this standard.[7]

Contemporaneous measures of substandard housing—certainly the ones applied in the 1940 census—do not do justice to the broad range of environmental issues that affect the health and welfare of inhabitants of such dwellings. Today we have a much clearer picture, thanks to the research findings reported by the World Health Organization, the National Centers for Disease Control and organizations such as the Robert Wood Johnson Foundation. To understand life in the segregated black neighborhoods, particularly in the overcrowded lower east side, that is, Black Bottom and Paradise Valley, it is useful to overlay a modern template of substandard conditions.[8]

A leading cause of chronic illness in the United States is allergies. Respiratory conditions such as asthma—the most common chronic disease among children—often develop or are exacerbated by conditions found in substandard housing. Leaking roofs, poor ventilation, dirty carpeting and pest infestations can lead to mold, dust mites and other allergens. Respiratory illnesses and some types of cancers can be traced to exposure to tobacco smoke, pollutants from faulty heating systems, natural gas cooking and asbestos dust released from insulation around boilers, furnaces and pipes.

Deteriorating paint in older homes, found in the nineteenth-century structures on the lower east side, is the primary source of lead exposure for children. Generally, homes built before 1978 often contain lead-based paint and lead in the plumbing system. Particularly in older homes, children ingest paint chips and inhale lead-contaminated dust. Housing can also be a source of exposure to various carcinogenic air pollutants.

Three young boys share a bed in a house in substandard condition. *Library of Congress.*

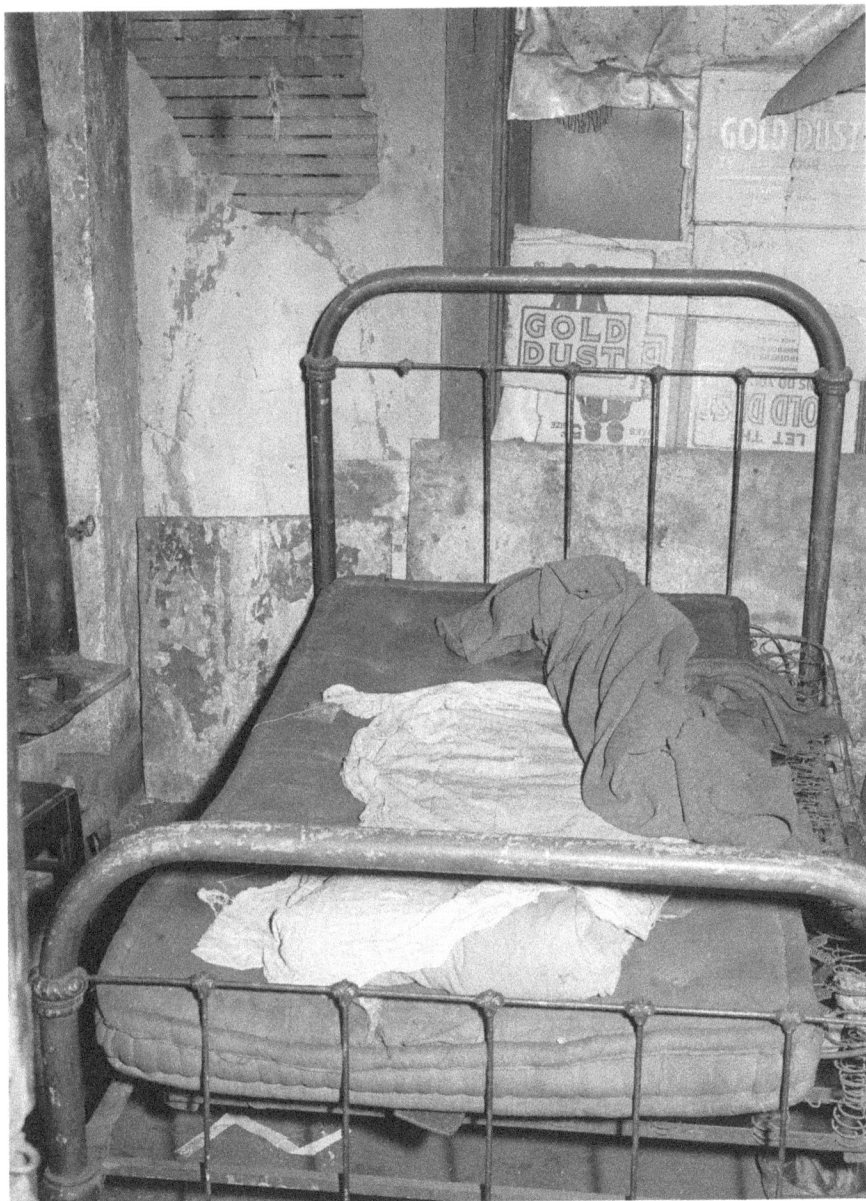

Bedroom in substandard house, with deteriorating and missing wall board to protect residents from the elements. *Library of Congress.*

Child plays on mound of debris in backyard of dilapidating housing structure. *Library of Congress.*

Older homes are not inherently less safe or conducive to physical injury. However, if these homes are not properly maintained, as in the case of homes and apartment buildings in Black Bottom and Paradise Valley, individuals are one slip or fall or burn from an emergency room visit. Unintentional home injuries naturally tend to be highest in the youngest and oldest age groups. Poorly maintained homes may have stairs in disrepair, loose or missing handrails, slippery surfaces—particularly in the kitchen and bathroom—inadequate lighting, missing or damaged window locks and guards and uncarpeted or concrete floors.

Fire- and scald-related injuries were a constant concern in the buildings on the lower east side. Practical, inexpensive smoke detectors were not widely available until well after World War II, and they would be less likely found in poorly maintained housing. In 1915, an individual had a one in ten chance of perishing in a house fire; a century later, the odds improved to one in one hundred. Scald burns and scald-related deaths tend to occur in such high-risk groups as children younger than four years and older persons with physical or mental disabilities. Scalds are associated with the lack of anti-scald devices for showerheads and faucets and defective water heater thermostats.

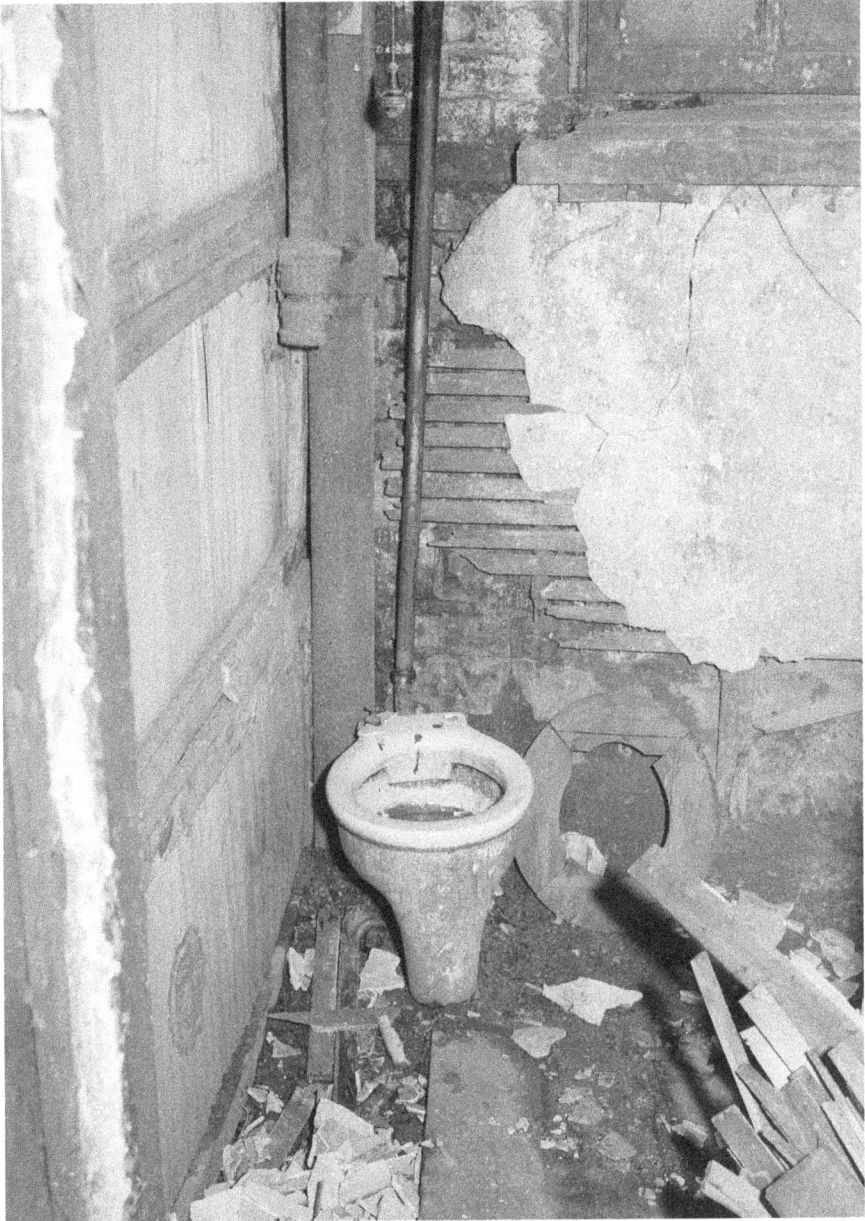

Toilet bowl in basement of substandard housing. *Library of Congress.*

Harold Ickes, secretary of the interior who promulgated the infamous neighborhood composition rule, reads communications in his office in Washington, D.C. *Library of Congress.*

Defects can be found even in homes originally built to code but not properly maintained. In the Eight Mile–Wyoming community, however, homes were not built to code. They were built by sweat equity, neighbor helping neighbor construct structures that would provide shelter from the elements, no matter the number or kind of defects in construction. When the FHA denied their residential loan, these urban settlers of the 1920s and 1930s made do with what materials were available and what construction skills they possessed, creating dangerous, potentially life-threatening living conditions. At the same time, on Detroit's near east side, in the enclaves of Black Bottom and Paradise Valley, African American residents were occupying poorly maintained houses and apartments. High rents absorbed so much of residents' income, owing to landlords exploiting the demand for housing in any condition, that funds were frequently unavailable for medical care, prescriptions and fresh food.

Acknowledging the need for safe, affordable housing for the defense plant workers, the Division of Defense Housing recommended the construction of one thousand government-financed family units, with two hundred of these units, on the recommendation of the Detroit Housing Commission, set aside for black occupancy. However, after dismissing the DHC's first recommendation, federal officials unilaterally decided on the second recommendation, a sparsely settled mixed neighborhood of twenty acres on the city's northeast side. Five city blocks to the northwest of this site at Nevada and Fenelon Streets was Conant Gardens, a subdivision of proud, middle-class black homeowners. The immediate community was served by Pershing High School and Atkinson School, both enrolling substantial numbers of black students. Polish immigrants had settled the area as well, though the largest concentration was due east, around St. Louis the King Church, less than a mile from the proposed housing site.

The problem created by the selection of the DHC's alternative site for black defense workers at Nevada and Fenelon was the application of the "Neighborhood Composition Rule," promulgated in 1933 by Interior Secretary Harold Ickes. Roosevelt knew that if he wanted to pass New Deal legislation, he had to appease largely segregationist Southern Democrats who voted as a bloc 85 percent of the time. The rule simply stated that new government-sponsored and -financed public housing should respect the

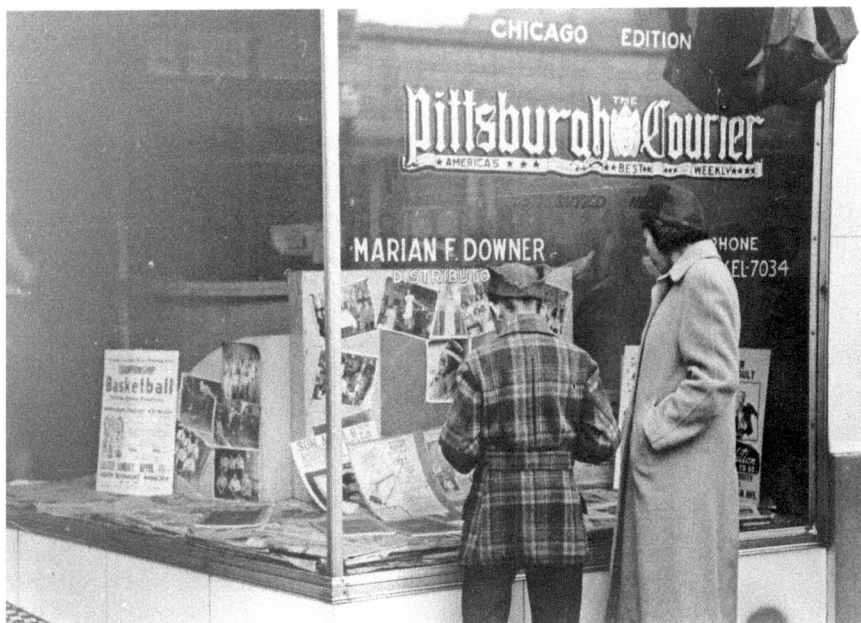

Storefront featuring current issues of the *Pittsburgh Courier*, America's largest and most influential weekly black newspaper of the era. *Library of Congress.*

racial composition of the existing neighborhood. If the neighborhood was white, new housing would remain white; if black, it would remain black. If mixed, theoretically it could remain mixed. However, in practice, new public housing in "mixed" neighborhoods was rarely, if ever, formally designated as mixed. Instead, local housing officials would establish the project as white or black, further segregating existing communities. Such was the case with the Sojourner Truth housing project.[9]

For the better part of a year, Detroit's major racial and ethnic factions argued over the efficacy of the Sojourner Truth defense housing project as a white or black project principally because of its location. It soon pulled in a variety of additional stakeholders, including the Division of Defense Housing Coordination, the Detroit Housing Commission, the Metropolitan Council of Churches, the Archdiocese of Detroit, the fiery pastor of St. Louis the King Parish, Conant Gardens Homeowners Association, local real estate developers, the newly established Fenelon Homeowners' Association, Mayor Jeffries, the UAW and last—and apparently least—the black defense workers for whom the project was originally designed. When Detroiter Walter Jackson declared his willingness to die rather than continue to be treated as a second-class citizen in such a matter as defense housing, he spoke for many African Americans throughout the nation.

As the Sojourner Truth housing controversy heated up in late fall of 1941 and extended into 1942, the U.S. military was forced to strategize for a war on two fronts: against Japan in the Pacific theater and against the Germans and Italians in Europe. For many African Americans, however, the concept of a war on two fronts soon conveyed a completely different meaning: conquering our enemies overseas while simultaneously defeating racism and discrimination at home.

One week after Pearl Harbor, the *Pittsburgh Courier*, the most widely read black newspaper in America, made the following front-page entreaty: "We call upon the President and Congress to declare war on Japan and racial prejudice. Certainly we should be strong enough to whip them both." The sentiment galvanized a national campaign during the war's first winter. On February 7, 1942—two months to the day after Pearl Harbor—the newspaper announced a national campaign to obliterate racism at home at the same time it defeated its enemies overseas. The "Double V" referred to the popular "V for Victory" slogan found in store and gas station windows across the nation. The second *V*, overlapping the first, represented the African American objective of achieving victory against discrimination and segregation on the homefront.[10]

Introduction

On the homefront, many African Americans were troubled by a war propaganda machine that openly denounced the doctrine of Aryan race superiority on the one hand but made segregation an official policy of the federal government on the other. The hypocrisy was palpable.

In Detroit, Sojourner Truth Homes would prove to be a test case of American ideals.

1
DETROIT'S SEGREGATED
NEIGHBORHOODS

The city of Detroit originated in 1701 as a fort and settlement along the Detroit River. A century later, the settlement was incorporated as a village and became the seat of government for the Michigan Territory. After fire completely destroyed their established structures, settlers saw an opportunity to re-plat the village and, eventually, reconstitute Detroit as a city in 1815. Detroit would become the state capital at the time of Michigan's admission to the Union in 1837 and remain so until the capital was moved to Lansing in 1847. From 1850 to 1910, Detroit's population grew from 21,019 to 465,766, but the city's black population remained in the range of 2 percent for the entire period, from 587 in 1850 to 5,741 in 1910.

As Detroit grew from a commercial center of a local agrarian economy to a regional industrial center, demographics changed dramatically. Beginning in 1910, the Great Migration of rural Southern whites and blacks to Detroit, fueled primarily by the promise of good jobs in factories such as in Henry Ford's auto assembly plant in Highland Park, put great pressure on the city's limited and highly segregated housing options. By 1920, in a city of now nearly 1 million, blacks numbered 40,838, or 4.11 percent.

Nonetheless, whatever difficulties they may have had in finding adequate housing in Detroit, African Americans had a double motive for abandoning the South. The plantation economy of the South—

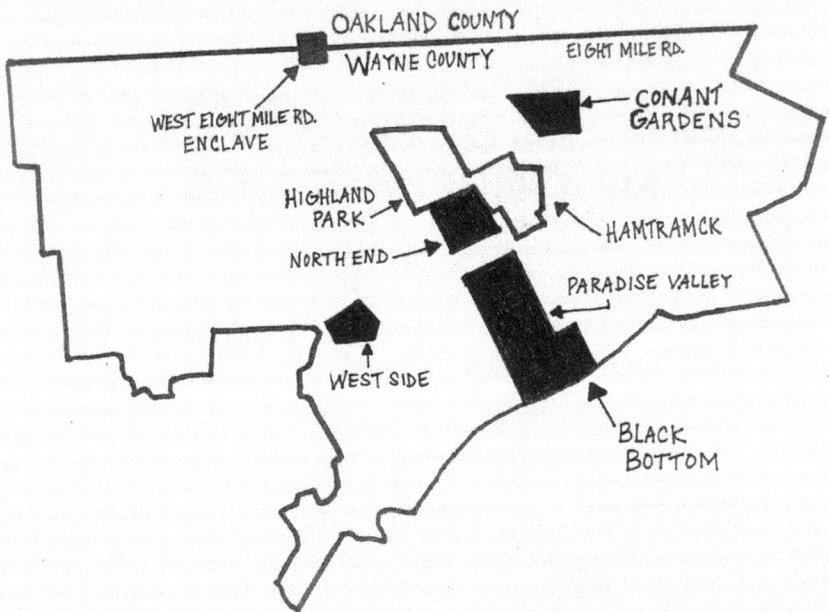

Pen-and-ink drawing depicting the six segregated black enclaves in the city of Detroit. *Author's collection.*

so dependent on sharecropping and tenant farming—offered little opportunity to advance beyond bare subsistence. Increased mechanization of farming, as well as the destructive impact of the boll weevil epidemic, created a labor oversupply, and what farm work was available now favored unemployed whites.

In addition to economics, blacks continued to suffer from terrorism in the white supremacist "Jim Crow" South. Although the KKK had technically been disbanded in 1869, it merely went underground. Violence against persons and property continued as tools of intimidation and social control. Voting rights were routinely suppressed through the imposition of poll taxes and literacy tests. The court system offered little relief from injustice, particularly involving racial disputes. And the bifurcated Southern educational system ("separate but equal") left black children with overcrowded classrooms and a shortage of textbooks, desks, blackboards and basic supplies—as well as with overworked, underpaid and often poorly trained teachers.[11] Still, leaving the South was a difficult and courageous act, and many African Americans who trekked north found work in large cities such as Mobile and Montgomery, Alabama, or Atlanta, Georgia, without ever having to cross the Mason-Dixon line.

BLACK BOTTOM

From 1910 to 1920, black migrants to Detroit would have been directed, almost universally, to Black Bottom, an area on the lower east side near the riverfront and bounded on the north by Gratiot Avenue, on the west by Brush Street, on the east by St. Aubin and on the south by the Grand Trunk Railroad Tracks. The area was thought to have been named for the rich loamy soil found along the shoreline of the river and not for any racial characteristics of its inhabitants. The fact is, Black Bottom had originally been settled by European immigrants two centuries prior. Through orderly succession, the area would be settled further and developed by an eastern European Jewish community. Even a century into Detroit's existence, in 1820, there were only 67 black residents out of a population of 1,422, or 4.7 percent. From 1820 to 1920, the overall size of Detroit would grow from a little more than a square mile, incorporating Black Bottom, to just over seventy-seven square miles in 1920, with large tracts of land annexed to the north and to the west.

Even as the city grew dramatically in both population and in land acquisition, black residents were confined largely to a single area, the districts of the near east side, with two to three hundred people per acre. By 1926, there was sufficient land in the city (now 139 square miles) to make life much more bearable for its one and a half million residents, but racially restrictive covenants sewn into the property deeds of Detroit's real estate transactions made migration from Black Bottom a legal nightmare for African Americans. And things would only get worse.[12]

Black Bottom was the first area of Detroit where African Americans could settle in large numbers. Before 1910, blacks integrated with many eastern and southern European immigrants, though blacks represented a small minority, living in relatively small wood-framed houses built close together on twenty- to thirty-foot lots. Originally constructed in the late 1800s, these houses occupied by blacks were clustered in an area bounded by Leland, Macomb, Brush and Hastings. After 1910, facing acute housing

Streetscape of Black Bottom, the largest and most crowded African American enclave in Detroit until the 1960s, when it was completely leveled as part of a major urban renewal effort in downtown Detroit. *Library of Congress.*

shortages signaled by the arrival of black migrants from the South, Black Bottom gradually expanded northward to Gratiot and eastward to St. Aubin. Housing conditions did not improve, however. Capricious landlords charged exorbitantly high rents for properties with unsanitary or unsafe conditions such as clogged plumbing and drainage, faulty electrical outlets, leaky roofs and unpredictable trash and rubbish pickups. In many cases, to make rent and accommodate new arrivals, boarders were taken in, further compromising healthy living space.

Blacks from the South were not only directed to Black Bottom but also drawn by its sense of community. The gravitational pull came from several

Alleyway in Black Bottom neighborhood, Detroit. *Library of Congress.*

sources, including its churches as well as its nascent commercial, political, social and cultural organizations. Front and center were its churches, particularly Second Baptist Church, the oldest black church in the Midwest, which had been an important Northern station along the Underground Railway for escaped slaves, and, later, New Bethel Baptist Church, led by the Reverend C.L. Franklin, at 4210 Hastings Street. During the 1920s and '30s, the African American enclave became a concentrated market for enterprising black businessmen who possessed the wherewithal to open and operate successful restaurants, barbershops, beauty parlors, drugstores and medical, dental and law offices.

Overhead view of backyard and house in Black Bottom, Detroit. *Library of Congress.*

One block east of St. Antoine, running north and south along the eastern edge of Black Bottom, was Hastings Street, which underwent a transformation in conformity to changing demographics and contemporary interests. In the late nineteenth century, Hastings Street originated as a commercial district where Jewish shopkeepers and peddlers purveyed such comestibles as milk, butter, beef, corn, beans, seasonal fruits and vegetables, as well as such dry goods as fabric and thread and related merchandise. After World War I, black entrepreneurs opened up new commercial avenues, including record stores, taverns, bowling alleys, furniture outlets, pool halls and blues clubs, in which such

Back of house in Black Bottom. *Library of Congress.*

important musicians as John Lee Hooker cut their teeth. By World War II, Hastings Street had also become a veritable boulevard of sin with notorious strip clubs, blind pigs and houses of ill repute.

PARADISE VALLEY

By the 1930s, a new and more upscale entertainment district was developing just north of Black Bottom and centered at the intersection of Adams and

St. Antoine. In 1935, the federal government broke ground on the Brewster Housing Project on St. Antoine between Adelaid and Mack Avenues. With First Lady Eleanor Roosevelt present for the groundbreaking, the new development offered some measure of relief from the overcrowding in Black Bottom. As a direct consequence, however, Paradise Valley's center of activity moved a block east to Hastings Street.[13]

The name of the area did not come by accident. Rollo S. Vest, theatrical editor for the local African American *Detroit Tribune*, ran a contest in the paper to name the fledgling district while promoting all the black owned and operated entertainment venues. As a booking agent for many of the local blues and jazz clubs, Vest recognized the value of branding, and when "Paradise Valley" was suggested, he seized upon it, and Paradise Valley was born. For eight consecutive years, from 1933 to 1940, readers of the *Tribune* had the opportunity to "vote" on a new "Mayor of Paradise Valley." In an extravagant inaugural ball held at the Graystone Ballroom, the new mayor was installed. A few of the more notable mayors included Sunnie Wilson, owner of the Forest Club; Chester Rentie, a talent booking agent who once managed jazz vocalist Betty Carter; and Roy H. Lightfoot, owner of the B&C Club, who happily became the first titleholder. Part of the mayor's duties were generally to represent and promote the Valley to the media, to act as master of ceremonies at neighborhood events and to coordinate local charity drives.

The value of the brand was not lost on local entrepreneurs. In 1941, for example, famed local fighter Joe Louis built the Paradise Bowl on Adams, just east of St. Antoine. The spacious facility featured a twenty-six-lane bowling alley, a roller-skating rink, a dining room and an ultramodern cocktail lounge. The most notable facility bearing the Paradise moniker was the Paradise Theater, so named by new owners Ben and Lou Cohen. The building was originally constructed in 1919 as the permanent home of the Detroit Symphony Orchestra (DSO). Renowned for its near perfect acoustics, the DSO was forced to sell the facility in 1939 owing to financial issues before moving to more modest quarters in the Masonic Temple. After a two-year period of operation as a moving picture and vaudeville house under the name of Town Theater, the Cohens stepped in, purchased the property and renamed it the Paradise Theater. The venue would become a charter member of the Chitlin Circuit, which included the Apollo Theater in Harlem; the Howard Theater in Washington, D.C.; the Uptown Theater in Philadelphia; the Royal Theater in Baltimore; and the Regal Theater in Chicago. In its heyday, the Paradise attracted such luminaries as Duke

Streetscape, Paradise Valley business district, just north of Black Bottom, Detroit. *Library of Congress.*

Ellington, Count Basie, Billie Holiday, Lionel Hampton, Nat King Cole, Ella Fitzgerald, Sarah Vaughn, B.B. King and scores of other blues and jazz legends.

The choice of hotel accommodations for prominent African Americans visiting Detroit invariably became the Gotham Hotel, located on the corner of John R and Orchestra Place. In 1943, John White and Irving Roane, two local black entrepreneurs, purchased the nine-story hotel from Danish businessman Albert Hartz. The Gotham soon became the choice of such black celebrities and cultural icons as Langston Hughes, Martin Luther King, Adam Clayton Powell, Thurgood Marshall and even the Harlem Globetrotters. The Gotham was known for its elegantly appointed guest

Pedestrians walking and shopping within the Paradise Valley business district. *Library of Congress.*

rooms and fine dining offered in the exquisite Ebony Room. It was hardly unusual to witness athletes and entertainers mingling with politicians and civil rights activists in the spacious lounge area in the front lobby.

Though much of the community continued to grow and prosper economically, there were significant issues working against its overall health and success. Overcrowded houses and apartments were bursting with the working poor and the unemployed, and illegal gambling in the form of Mafia-controlled numbers operations run out of local hotels such as the Norwood exploited Detroiters who could least afford to gamble away what was left after settling with their unscrupulous landlords. The elegant Gotham Hotel was not immune to such activity, as co-owner John White was widely known to be running a high-stakes gambling operation on the top floor of the hotel, frequented by both black and white politicians. The Detroit Police Department turned a blind eye to the operation for more than a decade before the FBI shut the hotel down in 1962 in what was the largest single gambling raid in Detroit history.

Paradise Valley is best remembered, however, for its numerous theaters, restaurants and nightclubs. Any night of the week, one could find superior entertainment at such venues as Jakes, the Tropicana, Club Harlem, the Flame Show Bar, Sportee's Lounge and the Horseshoe Bar. This concentrated area of black entrepreneurship, created ultimately by discrimination and segregation, would be obliterated by so-called urban renewal. Black Bottom and Paradise Valley would succumb to bulldozers during the 1950s to make way for the construction of Interstate 75 and housing redevelopment triggered by the passage of the Federal Housing Act of 1949.

NORTH END

Among Detroit's many historic neighborhoods, none is more reflective of the city's automotive manufacturing heritage than North End. The birthplace of the Model T, North End was once heralded as the most significant concentration of industry in the country, if not the world. North End was also home to a growing enclave of middle-class and working-class African Americans.

North End is bounded on the north by the alleyway between Woodland and Tennyson Streets that marks the boundary between the cities of Detroit and Highland Park, on the south by Interstate 94, on the east by the Canadian National tracks that also mark part of the boundary of the city of Hamtramck and on the west by Woodward Avenue.[14]

The City of Detroit annexed this roughly rectangular piece of land from Hamtramck Township in 1891. The moniker "North End" likely derives from the fact that at the time of annexation this 393-acre parcel represented the city's northernmost boundary. One year later, Arden Park became the earliest platted residential development within the district. Planned as a luxury residential community, Arden Park remains even today one of the most desirable and architecturally diverse communities in the city proper, including examples of Tudor, Colonial, Renaissance and Prairie styles.

By 1900, many of Detroit's business and industrial leaders built homes in Arden Park, including John Dodge, Frederick Fisher, Clayton and Albert Grinnell and J.L. Hudson. During the next two decades, single-family homes and apartments dominated the local landscape, particularly south of Holbrook and north of East Grand Boulevard. Along such north and south residential streets as John R, Brush, Beaubien and Oakland developed many attached row houses reminiscent of East Coast urban architecture. In many instances, neighborhood businesses—bakeries, butcher shops, cleaners, hardware stores, millineries and so on—occupied the first floors of these structures. By 1920, the city had constructed eight new schools to accommodate the growing influx of settlers.

Immediately south of East Grand Boulevard is Milwaukee Junction, so named because of its location at the intersection of the Detroit, Grand Haven and Milwaukee Railway and the Chicago, Detroit and Canada Grand Trunk Junction Railroad. Detroit's industrial growth can be traced, in no small part, to this sub-district that provided ready access for factories to the national rail network while keeping these industrial sites relatively isolated from the city's residential areas. By 1920, Milwaukee Junction had become the primary hub for the automobile industry as such companies as Ford, Fisher Body, Packard, Studebaker and more than a dozen others flocked to the area. On the corner of Woodward and East Grand Boulevard, Ford built an impressive Albert Kahn–designed sales and service facility in 1909. Other companies followed suit.

Milwaukee Junction was also home to the Jam Handy Organization. Founded in 1911 by Henry Jamison "Jam" Handy, the company produced in its studio complex on East Grand Boulevard promotional and educational movies as well as training films for the armed forces. By 1935, the company employed over four hundred writers, directors and trade craft workers. Famed animator Max Fleischer created the animated movie *Rudolph the Red-Nosed Reindeer* in Handy's studio.

In the years prior to World War I, a massive influx of immigrants arrived in Detroit, particularly from eastern and central Europe. Many were working-class Jewish immigrants who settled in the North End to work in the automobile and related industries and to reestablish the dense network of religious and social institutions to which they were accustomed in Europe.

The infamous Purple Gang, a Mafia-style Jewish crime organization, was based primarily in the Brush Park neighborhood. A few blocks away, on the corner of Oakland and Hague and on the site of a former dance hall, Harry

Ford Piquette Plant in North End, Detroit, where Henry Ford rolled out Model Ts and experimented with a moving assembly line before shifting operations to a much larger production facility in Highland Park, Detroit. *Author's collection.*

Metzger Jr., a Purple Gang associate, opened the Oakland Health Club in 1930. (Known today as the Schvitz Health Club—Yiddish for "sweat"—this Russian-style bathhouse is still in operation.) The Purple Gang likely spent a great deal of time in the bathhouse, evidenced by the numerous bullet holes in a painting in the lobby. The baths may have served as a watering hole for the gang during Prohibition because of its status as a private club, which placed it outside of direct police scrutiny.

During this same period, small concentrations of African Americans lived in Highland Park and Hamtramck, on north Russell Street and near Milwaukee Junction. Over the next decade, Oakland Avenue became a hub for black musical innovation, making it a major blues and jazz scene. Oakland Avenue functioned as an extension of Hastings Street to the south. This avenue hosted numerous music venues and black-owned businesses, such as the Apex Bar at 7649 Oakland and Phelps Lounge at 9000 Oakland. Blues artist John Lee Hooker established himself at the Apex in the early '40s as the principal evening act after working a full day as a janitor at one of Detroit's downriver steel mills. One of Hooker's signature songs, "Boom," was inspired by his time at the Apex: "I would

47

Jam Handy Building on East Grand Boulevard, Detroit. *Author's collection.*

Oakland Health Club, offering a steam room, sauna and private lounge for members only in North End, Detroit. Frequent hangout for Detroit's infamous Purple Gang. *Author's collection.*

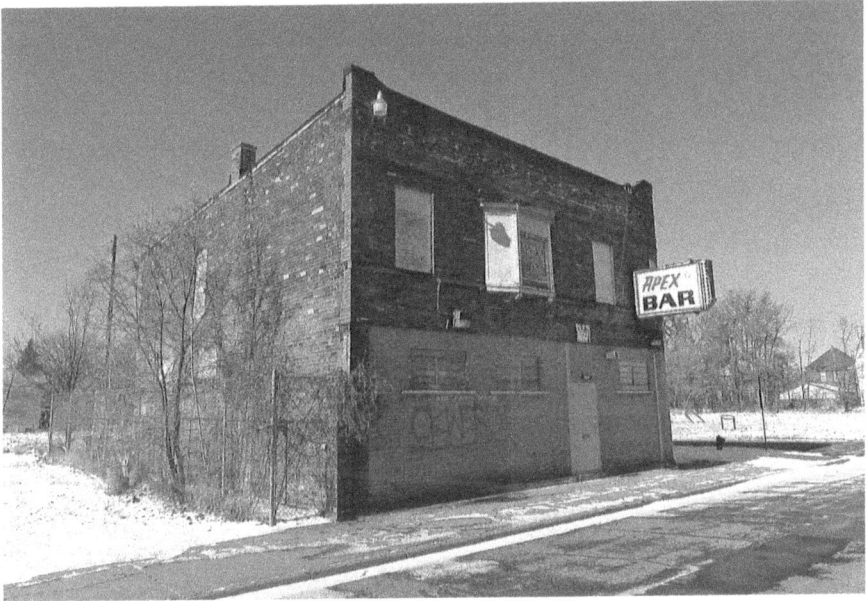

Apex Bar at 7649 Oakland Street, North End, Detroit. Favorite venue during the war years of legendary blues performer John Lee Hooker. *Author's collection.*

never be on time. I always would be late comin' in. Willa the bartender always had the same things to say to me, 'Boom, you late again.' I said, 'Hmm, that's a song.'" Likewise, the Phelps Lounge, previously the Bizerte Jazz Bar, was a showcase for acts like James Brown, Etta James, B.B. King and Little Richard.

By 1940, the black population of North End had climbed to 40 percent. Ten years later, population peaked with 51,709 residents, and African Americans were significantly in the majority. North End had firmly established itself as a black enclave in an otherwise highly segregated city. And so the pattern of racial succession occurred in the transfer of real estate between Jews and blacks on North End, just as it had occurred throughout Black Bottom and Paradise Valley. As Jewish residents crossed Woodward Avenue in their generational move to and through northwest Detroit, black citizens were there to gradually establish a foothold and create an enclave.

"OLD WEST SIDE"

"Old West Side," as former residents called it, was yet another African American enclave within the city of Detroit centered at Tireman and Grand River. The area was actually composed of several neighborhoods. The boundaries were Grand River to the east, Buchanan to the south, Tireman to the north and Epworth to the west. Residents who lived west of Grand Boulevard typically worked in plants, were self-employed businessmen and women or were employed by the government or various other industries throughout the city. Residents of Scotten, Firwood and Boxwood were more typically professionals, such as physicians, dentists, attorneys and morticians. Aside from the small enclave at Eight Mile and Wyoming, blacks were unwelcome west of Woodward until well after World War II. Tireman became a visible barrier between black and white, solidified legally by racially restrictive covenants and unscrupulous real estate agents who steered clientele to properties by the color of their skin.[15]

Westsiders, in the main, were working-class individuals until World War II, when the huge labor shortage opened up many new job opportunities for blacks. A new African American middle class began to emerge by the end of the war, and the west side of Detroit reflected this gradual transformation.

But in the 1920s and '30s, blacks on the west side of Woodward, as elsewhere, had limited employment options. The largest employer was the Ford Motor Company, followed by the Kelsey Hayes Wheel Company. Both the Michigan Central Railroad and the U.S. Post Office did employ a number of blacks prior to World War II. General Motors, on the other hand, had a large Cadillac facility on Detroit's west side but did not start hiring African Americans until the war. Other west side businesses and factories, such as the Lincoln plant on Livernois and Awrey Bakery on Tireman, employed thousands of Detroiters between 1920 and 1950, but very few were African American.

Like the other segregated enclaves of Detroit, such racial concentration created business opportunities for the more resourceful. A large number of minority-owned businesses cropped up on the West Side catering primarily to a black clientele. Arthur G. Bennett, for example, was the first African American owner-operator of a Shell Oil Station in the Detroit area, located on West Warren and Junction, across from the Granada Theater, and he drew strong community support for many years. Florine Hawkins, a Georgia transplant, began her career in Detroit by selling shoes door to door on the west side. She later expanded her line to include dresses, lingerie and linens. On July 3, 1947, Florine opened the Hawkins Apparel Shop on West Warren. Other families worked together to build businesses, such as the Thompson Brothers' Shoe Repair and Store, Peterson and Son Appliances, Jones Brothers Cleaners and Hatters, Hamilton Brothers Auto Service and G.W. Lloyd and Sons Movers.

West Side physicians found it difficult to practice their craft in the 1920s and '30s, as a number of Detroit hospitals denied their patients' admittance, and no black medical practitioners were appointed to hospital staffs. In 1918, local black physicians built their own hospital, Dunbar Hospital, at Frederick and St. Antoine on the city's near east side. Physicians and dentists living or maintaining offices on the west side from 1920 to 1950 included James Young (the first African American to be appointed by Mayor Frank Murphy as Detroit's city physician), D.J. Grimes, D.J. Graham, A.B. Cleage, James Brewer, William H. Lawson, A.L. Turner, John Bargyh, Lloyd Bailer and many others. Curiously, Betty Ann Graham, granddaughter of Dr. James Young, was the last baby to be delivered at Dunbar on August 26, 1929, with Dr. Young in attendance.

Another noteworthy Westsider was William Hiram Lawson, OD, who lived on Firwood Avenue for over sixty-eight years. Originally from Windsor, Canada, Dr. Lawson moved with his parents to Detroit as a child but returned to Canada to attend the Toronto School of Optometry. He subsequently opened an office in Windsor but, after taking and passing the Michigan State Board examination, returned to Detroit as the first African American optometrist in the United States and Canada. In 1944, Dr. Lawson was joined in his practice by his son, William E. Lawson, who—at age twenty-one—was the youngest optometrist ever passed by the board.

Living in a city as segregated as Detroit, West Side residents had to use creativity and resourcefulness to provide recreational experiences for their families. Off limits to Westsiders were many of Detroit's hotels, restaurants and entertainment venues. Despite these restrictions, there were opportunities to enjoy picnicking, swimming and boating at Rouge Park or on Belle Isle. During the winter, nearby Northwestern High School flooded a field for outdoor ice skating. Another popular venue was the Lothrop Branch of the Detroit Public Library on West Grand Boulevard.

Black professionals were looking for a place to relax and network with their community peers. Rejected by the all-white Detroit Athletic Club and the Detroit Club, Raymond H. Menard and Julian Archer founded the Nacirema ("American" spelled backward) Club in 1922. The club purchased a two-story brick house and converted the property to a clubhouse for men

Nacirema Club, 6118 Thirtieth Street, Detroit, Michigan. Building purchased by African American professionals to serve as social club for "West Siders." *Author's collection.*

only. (Women would be admitted to membership in 1998.) The Nacirema Club enjoys the distinction of being the first African American social club in Michigan, and its building at 6118 Thirtieth Street was listed in the National Register of Historic Places in 2011.

EIGHT MILE–WYOMING

In 1920, the City of Detroit's fairly regular and rapid annexation of land had not yet extended to Eight Mile Road. A new subdivision, called Garden Homes, was one of the few areas in or near Detroit that was open for sale to African Americans, and lots were selling briskly. Precious few whites had settled in this area of unannexed land, and the many blacks who did were beginning to form a community of like-minded pioneers.

The land at issue was part of a much larger parcel owned by Henry G. Stevens, a Detroit philanthropist and first president of the Detroit Urban League, an organization founded on principles of racial harmony, if not full integration. Stevens would sell the land to real estate developers intent on breaking the parcel up into small, affordable lots. Once purchased, it was hoped, construction would begin on housing that would absorb some of the pressure overcrowding and blight were creating on Detroit's near east side. The interurban streetcar line serviced the new area of development, so transportation for employment to and from the city did not seem to be an issue, though the streetcar stop was nearly a mile from the subdivision.[16]

Since banks charged private contractors who were willing to build in the area higher interest rates, few residents were able to afford these professional services. Instead, many residents built the main floor as a foundation and then set vertical poles in each corner to support what amounted to a large tent with walls made up of whatever malleable materials they could find. And still others constructed shacks, piece by piece, as lumber was purchased and scrap material became available locally.

Social workers dispatched to the area from the newly formed Detroit Urban League were distressed by the conditions under which residents lived their daily lives. With neither running water nor electricity, these migrants, it was feared, had "reverted" to their Southern roots. They were, in fact, recoiling from the unhealthy and inhospitable conditions within Black Bottom, where private space and good nutrition were at a premium. Here homesteaders engaged in subsistence farming, decorative gardening and small livestock breeding, particularly chicken, hogs and goats. Unpurchased lots became community gardens. If they were to be rejected in their efforts at integrating with Detroit's white majority, then they would need to become self-sufficient. The unannexed land on both sides of Eight Mile and Wyoming created an opportunity for blacks to reject the transient nature of life on Detroit's near east side and to develop a family-oriented community close enough to the big city for employment purposes but far enough away to avoid its inequities and iniquities.

In a sense, the Eight Mile–Wyoming community can only be fully understood as two halves of a larger one-square-mile whole, the present half-square-mile Royal Oak Township north of Eight Mile and the half-square mile of neighborhoods to the south that were annexed by the City of Detroit in 1923. Although both communities have unique historical moments, they are aligned closely by race, by culture and by shared experiences.[17]

Both before and after annexation, the community was well served by a black-owned commercial strip along Eight Mile Road. On the Detroit side, there was the Lett store, Worthy's, McCuller's Community Store, Charlie Rich's Pool Hall, Alfred Davis's Funeral Home and Thomas

Home built on Birwood Street in segregated West Eight Mile enclave. Children playing on mound of dirt next to house. Note the six-foot concrete wall in background. *Library of Congress.*

"Doc" Washington's drugstore. Doc also owned Uncle Tom's BBQ. There were white-owned businesses as well, including Jim Dolan's, an Atlantic & Pacific Supermarket in Royal Oak Township, Sam's Gas Station and Cockfield Funeral Home. Alice Newman recalled how her father, Jimmy Cain, managed several successful businesses on the north side of Eight Mile Road, including producing stage shows where he shared the stage as a musician. Newman vividly recalled performing in his shows as a dancer, earning a quarter a week. Perhaps her clearest and most colorful memory, however, was the hot dog stand her father operated on Parkside and Eight Mile Road called Jimmy's, which became a popular hangout for young people. Hot dogs and soda pop were a nickel each, and a bowl of chili was a quarter. When her grandmother felt up to baking, single slices of sweet potato pie sold out quickly. Local kids enjoyed the varieties of gum and candy available but especially loved playing the slot machine in the back, with its spinning lemons and oranges and other colorful fruit.

Considering that there were fewer than five hundred African American–owned businesses registered in the entire state of Michigan in 1929, Eight

Mile–Wyoming was a haven for black entrepreneurs. During the early 1930s, the black-owned businesses fronting Eight Mile Road were wiped out when the state highway department decided to widen the road. The local businesses tried but failed in court to stop the proposed project, and so another chapter of black entrepreneurship was lost to the annals of local history.

Immediately to the west of the Eight Mile–Wyoming community was a large parcel of undeveloped land. In 1940, a real estate developer approached the FHA with plans to develop the property that commenced on the easement between Birwood and Mendota Streets and extended westward. His application for FHA insurance on bank loans for his whites-only clientele was initially rejected because the proposed project bordered directly on a "hazardous" neighborhood, as defined by the Home Owners Loan Corporation's City Survey Program. The FHA was reluctant to insure bank loans on such properties because racially mixed areas, the agency reasoned, were likely to stir confrontation, lead to violence and jeopardize the fiscal soundness of the investment. Undaunted, the developer approached the FHA a second time with a new and novel

Wall built by developer in 1941 to "protect" his real estate interests. The Birwood Wall, still standing today, stretches from Eight Mile Road three blocks south to Pembroke Avenue. *Library of Congress.*

55

Children, oblivious to the deeper significance of the concrete wall behind them, pose for a picture on a sunny day in August 1941. *Library of Congress.*

proposal: he would construct a wall, six feet high and one foot thick, between the "hazardous" neighborhood east of Birwood and the proposed new development. The FHA agreed to the compromise. The Birwood Wall today stands as a monument to federal government complicity with racial segregation in the city of Detroit.

CONANT GARDENS

In northeast Detroit, Conant Gardens became one of the first urban land tracts available for African Americans to actually build their own new homes, with FHA-approved loans, instead of having to purchase from an already existing stock of houses previously owned by European immigrants. Bounded by Seven Mile Road, Ryan Road, Nevada and Conant, the land was originally owned by Shubael Conant, a staunch abolitionist who founded the Detroit Anti-Slavery Society. Though he never married or had children, he instructed his heirs—various nephews—to disallow the insertion of any racially restrictive covenants into the deeds on land put up for sale. Thus, one by one, African American families purchased lots within the tract and built a variety of modest homes—frame, brick and a combination of brick and second-floor wood veneer.[18]

Aptly named Conant Gardens, this new community of African Americans transformed backyards into vegetable gardens of green beans, tomatoes, okra, collard and mustard greens, squash, peas, corn, cabbage and rhubarb. Forming borders around both house and garden were phlox, zinnias, gladiolas, marigolds, begonias, petunias and asters. Adjacent vacant lots also became gardens as they awaited homes to be built. New neighbors were quickly schooled on the merits of one particular grass seed over another.

Steady rather than specific kinds of employment, well-groomed lawns and brightly painted houses seemed to be the common denominators among families. Living alongside one another were doctors, accountants, postal workers, teachers, Ford factory workers, civil service employees, dentists, lawyers, sanitation workers and self-employed shopkeepers. Empty lots soon became construction sites, and existing residents began to be concerned about quality control. To ensure that property values would hold or even appreciate, a Conant Gardens Community Association was formed. The neighborhood attorneys drew up bylaws and regulations that addressed residential structures, habitation and commercial properties. Only single-family dwellings with one outer (front) entrance would be permitted. Occupancy was limited to one family. Commercial establishments were prohibited within the community but allowed on the periphery. Farm animals were prohibited.

Conant Gardens survived the Depression, but not without considerable cost to the community. As unemployment took its toll, some homeowners missed payments on their properties and were forced to sell or walk away. Franklin D. Roosevelt's New Deal work programs and welfare assistance provided many Detroiters with a lifeline. Within Conant Gardens, filling dozens of vacant lots and paving the numerous dirt roads were placed on hold until the conclusion of World War II, at which time homebuilding resumed and all the streets were eventually paved.

The children of the community were served by Atkinson or Courville Elementary Schools, Cleveland Intermediate School and Pershing High School. One Cleveland student, Mildred Benson Scott, recalls that just before graduation in 1936, a classroom picture was taken with all six black students

Streetscape, Conant Gardens segregated neighborhood enclave in northeast Detroit, just four city blocks from Sojourner Truth Homes housing project, the site of the February 28 riot. *Author's collection.*

seated by the photographer on the bottom row, allowing for white families to easily "sanitize" the class photo by excising the bottom two inches. Located at Seven Mile and Ryan Roads, Pershing High School opened its doors on September 3, 1930, as a single school unit. A scarcity of funding prevented the city school system from constructing Pershing's auditorium, gymnasium and swimming pool until 1952.

Against this backdrop of established African American communities within the city limits of Detroit came a huge influx of black Southerners seeking employment in the defense industry beginning in 1939. From 1940 to 1950, Detroit's black population doubled from 149,119 to 300,506. Although 186,000 single-family homes were constructed in metropolitan Detroit during the 1940s, only 1,500 were available for black occupancy. The Second Great Migration put tremendous strain on the six segregated communities. Garages, attics, cellars and storefronts were converted into makeshift housing to accommodate the influx of daily arrivals.

2

VENTURING OUTSIDE THE ENCLAVE

D espite the level of support and security African Americans enjoyed within the confines of a particular enclave in Detroit, anger and anxiety were constants for many African Americans. Black resentment had deepened not only because of the worsening wartime housing crisis and employment discrimination but also because of particular policies and practices that arose during the war. The Red Cross, for example, barred black donors as early as December 1941 and relented later, only reluctantly, by accepting—but segregating—African American blood donations. In the U.S. Navy, furthermore, blacks were typically given the most menial jobs on board; the Marine Corps would not even accept African Americans. The indignities went on.

TRANSPORTATION

Venturing outside the enclave to go to work, to shop for groceries, to go to school, to meet doctor appointments or to simply enjoy a picnic at an integrated municipal park, like Belle Isle, was a daily challenge. The wartime shortage of automobiles, not to mention mandatory gas rationing, created crowded conditions on the buses and streetcars. Newly arriving blacks and whites from the South were competing not only for jobs in Detroit but also for space on public conveyances. Southern whites, who had journeyed north for the same jobs, were now having to adjust behaviors to accommodate an unaccustomed reality. Social psychologist Roger Brown, who was a high school student in Detroit at the time, recalls the buildup of tension preliminary to the 1943 riot; there were strains on Detroit's preexisting black population but also, of a different nature, "for the Southern whites who had come to Detroit for war-related work and were not accustomed to the degree of equality that prevailed there, to unsegregated public transportation and partially unsegregated recreational facilities."[19]

One of the remarkable aspects of this period in Detroit's transportation history is the level of African American participation in its day-to-day operations. Prior to 1922, few blacks found employment anywhere within Detroit's transportation system, except for "laying tracks and in various menial jobs." Following the election of James Couzens as mayor, however, the black community found a sympathetic ear at city hall, and through the offices of the Detroit Urban League, significant strides were made in

One of several newly built bus trolleys to service high demand for public transportation in 1940s Detroit. *Walter P. Reuther Library, Archives of Labor and Urban Affairs, Wayne State University.*

African American recruitment and hiring. For the first time, blacks were driving and maintaining buses and trolleys, though not without significant backlash from white passengers, who complained about good civil service jobs being taken from them. By 1942, the dramatic influx of Southern blacks and whites—both of whom were culturally different from native Detroit blacks and whites—was putting tremendous strain on the public transportation system. City residents without cars or the fuel to operate them were dependent on public transportation to take them to various employment centers scattered across the nearly 140 square miles of the city. The number of passengers on the combined bus and trolley lines increased from 30,811,660 in 1940 to 34,171,174 in 1941 and 45,033,989 in 1942.[20] Racial confrontation gradually escalated from verbal to physical on the overcrowded and fully integrated bus service, exacerbated by deeply ingrained prejudices of transplanted Southerners. The battle lines for social equality were being drawn during the war in the city's public transportation system.

THE WORKING ENVIRONMENT

The combined pull of good job prospects in the industrial North and the push from deplorable social conditions in the Jim Crow South became the tipping point for tens of thousands of blacks who made Detroit a primary destination between 1910 and 1950. The farm-to-city movement did not exclude intermediate stops in Southern cities like Birmingham, Memphis and Atlanta, all of which experienced significant population growth between 1910 and 1930. But for large numbers of black families, the magnet of real opportunity lay farther north.

The First World War brought about employment opportunities to blacks heretofore almost completely unobtainable. Previously in Detroit, African Americans were engaged almost entirely in personal service occupations—janitor, porter, elevator operator, domestic, hotel waiter and so forth. From a purely business point of view, factory owners or superintendents were thought to be protecting their investments. The idea of using blacks in any appreciable number was considered ludicrous— the operating theory regarding blacks in the labor forces was that they were irremediably slothful and inefficient and that they could not stand the intensive demands of Northern industry. Above all, it was believed that black and white did not mix on the factory floor, whether the white laborer was native or foreign born. Now with the labor vacuum created by the wartime curb on immigration and therefore immigrant labor, need created opportunity.

Blacks migrating to Detroit for work found employment opportunities both during and after the war, although they suffered extreme levels of discrimination with respect to the nature of the work and opportunities for advancement. Factory foremen, regardless of the specific industry in Detroit, offered the black job applicant the hottest, dirtiest, noisiest, most physically exhausting and most dangerous jobs on the floor. Starting on the bottom more often led to staying on the bottom. Discrimination in wages earned or hours worked did not really apply. Wages and hours were more a function of the kind of work needed to be done. The worst jobs were paid the worst hourly wage. No white worker wanted these jobs and would have been forced into them only when necessary and, it was expected, only temporarily.

The automobile industry absorbed large numbers of black job applicants, though not equally among car companies or even within different plants of the same company. The first factories to integrate were Ford, Briggs and Dodge. Overall, two-thirds of blacks hired were classified as unskilled laborers, while the same was true for only one-fourth of whites. Such unskilled jobs included sweeping, tending the furnace and iron smelting and pouring; semiskilled positions, when they were available, were limited to the most dangerous or undesirable, such as sand blaster, shear operator or heater.

Ford Motor Company, the largest single employer of African Americans, attempted to hire blacks in proportion to their presence in metropolitan Detroit's labor force. In 1926, this number was ten thousand. Ford attempted to disperse these black employees across all departments and occasionally even offered supervisory positions. Vertical movement within the company, on a happenstance basis, was atypical. A conscious policy among industry leaders, including Ford Motor Company executives, guided hiring and placement decisions: blacks could work harmoniously with whites so long as they knew their place.

In 1916, Forrester B. Washington and Henry G. Stevens opened the first Detroit Urban League (DUL) office, an affiliate of the National Urban League (NUL), which had been created earlier to solve some of the many problems black migrants from the South were experiencing in the urban industrial centers. Its mission gradually expanded to include seeking employment and housing opportunities while offering a variety of social services, including healthcare and recreation.[21]

Part of Detroit's massive Packard Plant on the east side, employing over thirty-five thousand individuals who produced naval engines as well as Rolls-Royce aircraft engines. *Library of Congress.*

Within the factory environment, blacks faced racial abuse, shop floor violence and horrendous working conditions resulting in long-term health issues. Racial abuse took many forms, from foreman and co-workers hurling insults and racial epithets to speed-up demands and accusations of laziness cast in particularly offensive stereotypical language. Shop floor violence before, during and after shift change was not uncommon, particularly in the rare instance when an African American was promoted to a position whites felt they were passed over for.

Health issues surfaced most dramatically in the actual working conditions on the shop floor. Blacks were subjected to the dirtiest, most labor intensive and most hazardous areas of the plant. Each area or department, however, had its particular set of health issues. In the River Rouge Plant's massive blast furnaces and foundries, or in the toxic air environment of the paint shops, blacks were most often found.

The workplace environment for African Americans contributed to a disproportionate degree of exposure to dangerous toxic elements. In the paint shops, for example, black workers were exposed to solvents, additives and other chemicals used in the vehicle painting process, leading to increased risk of several kinds of occupation-related cancers such as lung, bladder and pancreatic cancer. In the blast furnaces and foundries, workers were exposed to molten metal explosions, heat exhaustion and stroke, severe burns and eye disorders from ultraviolet or infrared radiation emanating from the molten metal.

Other areas of the factory offered constant exposure to asbestos, as the heating pipes and water pipes were wrapped in a fabric containing the deadly silicate mineral. Asbestos was also used in the manufacture of brake shoes and clutch plates. Lung scarring and many different cancers— including lung, colon, esophageal and stomach cancer—were the outcomes of such exposure, although symptoms might not develop for years. A union benefit representative once claimed, with unmistakable gallows humor, that he could determine what department employees worked in from reading the death certificates.

The path of employment for blacks in Detroit lay first in the automobile factories and foundries. Gradually, officials of the major Detroit utilities—Detroit Edison, Michigan Consolidated Gas and Michigan Bell Telephone—revised their hiring standards and began to hire qualified blacks. After this, banks and department stores followed suit. National Bank of Detroit and Detroit Bank and Trust were among the first Detroit-area banks to hire African Americans. J.L. Hudson Company, Detroit's premier department store, placed black women on its elevators, and the DUL saw this as a major opportunity for African Americans to serve as public ambassadors. Crowley's Department Store next door soon began to place black women on its elevators as well. Gradually, a few black women were offered opportunities to work as salespersons. Their success led to further opportunities.[22]

THE STATE OF AFRICAN AMERICAN HEALTHCARE

Regardless of where in Detroit one received medical treatment, racial discrimination and segregation of services helped to explain why African Americans suffered the worst healthcare treatment, the worst health status and the worst health outcomes of any race or ethnic group being treated. Racial discrimination in one form or another permeated every aspect of healthcare, from discriminatory hiring practices with respect to doctors, nurses, orderlies and other clinical staffing to inferior treatment for various conditions or even withholding treatment for those conditions. Racial discrimination even affected the insurance billing industry, which routinely accepted, rejected or adjusted claims based on the race of the claimant and paid different rates to the provider of services based on the same.

The enormous gap between the health of Detroit's white and black residents in 1940 is reflected in the overall mortality rates (8.0 versus 11.3 per thousand), infant mortality rates (2.9 versus 3.6 per thousand) and maternal mortality (36.0 versus 50.8 per thousand). Except for accidents and cancer, African Americans registered significantly higher rates in such categories as heart disease, pneumonia and venereal disease. When one factors in that whites possessed more vehicles and lived, on average, ten years longer than their black counterparts, the higher accident and cancer diagnoses are understandable. Especially troubling, however, was that the death rate due to tuberculosis (168 per hundred thousand) was seven times that of whites statewide.

A decade later, the statistical correlation between race and selective diseases remained. In 1951, the Detroit Urban League studied wholly manageable diseases such as pneumonia and tuberculosis that afflicted blacks disproportionately due to discriminatory hospital and clinical practices in Detroit. To dramatize the "brutal callousness" to which African Americans were subjected, the DUL cited the following case study as representative:

> On October 8, 1951, at 7:30 p.m., Mrs. Roosevelt Walton, a Negro mother, brought her baby to Dr. Thornton's office in Ecorse. The doctor gave the child immediate attention because it was evident the child was seriously ill. He diagnosed the case as bronchial pneumonia and urged the mother to take her baby to CHILDREN'S HOSPITAL immediately as the child needed oxygen.
>
> Mrs. Walton arrived at CHILDREN'S HOSPITAL at 8:05 p.m. and gave the receptionist a letter she had gotten from Dr. Thornton indicating the nature of the case. Mrs. Walton was told to wait her turn. After waiting over an hour, she again approached the receptionist but was told again to wait. Mrs. Walton became hysterical as she saw the condition of her baby become worse. A gentleman in the waiting room came over to look at the baby. He screamed, "The baby is dying." The nurses ran to the baby and took the child to the examining room. But it was too late. The baby had died.[23]

The origins of the African American healthcare crisis can be traced back to the population explosion in the run-up to World War I and the segregationist mentality of whites supervising medical education and clinical training and administering the city's hospitals and clinics. Obtaining a medical education as a black undergraduate was fraught with barriers designed to discourage even the bravest souls. Admission locally to Wayne State University's Medical School was normally selective, but for African Americans it was nearly impossible. At that time, Wayne would take one black entrant and maybe two Jewish entrants per year. Most did not bother to apply. For the few who did, even an extraordinary record of undergraduate accomplishment might be insufficient for serious consideration. Instead, most had to leave the state to attend institutions where their applications would be taken more seriously, such as historically black schools like Meharry Medical College or Howard University College of Medicine. Afterward, obtaining a hospital internship or medical residency became another gauntlet. For a black physician in Detroit to become a surgeon, he or she became a resident at one of the black hospitals, where, in many instances, a large patient load of severely ill people was waiting. Municipal hospitals, which operated on a black patient quota system, would often admit blacks whose situations promised to be useful teaching cases and transfer the remaining to the small black hospitals—if they had space to take them.

With rare exception, black physicians who applied for staff positions and admitting privileges to both municipal and to proprietary hospitals were rejected. Furthermore, proprietary hospitals rejected black patients wholesale; municipal hospitals operated on a quota system. If one had seriously ill patients, one had to persuade a white colleague to admit them to the hospital. Such a policy had serious consequences. As Lionel Swan, MD, recalled:

> *I had called a white colleague who agreed to hospitalize a woman who I diagnosed as possible kidney failure. When she reached the hospital and her husband, not knowing the name of the white doctor, stated her doctor was Dr. Swan, the admitting clerk recognizing the name as that of a black doctor obviously not on the hospital staff, refused to admit the patient. She died shortly thereafter on the same day. There was a universal outcry of condemnation of the clerk's action, but nothing was done except possibly a promise to use better discretion in the future.*[24]

Dunbar Hospital, 580 Frederick Street, serving Detroit's African American community at a time when general admission to local hospitals was greatly restricted for people of color. *Author's collection.*

To provide better training for black physicians and more comprehensive care for black patients, a handful of physicians opened private black-owned hospitals. The first was Dunbar Hospital, named after the famous black poet Paul Laurence Dunbar. Thirty black physicians, led by Dr. James W. Ames, purchased the old Charles W. Warren house just west of Woodward Avenue on Frederick Street and formed the Allied Medical Society to promote the health and well-being of the African American community. In the years following, more than a dozen black proprietary hospitals opened in Detroit, including Kirkwood, Edyth K. Thomas, Trinity, Burton Mercy and, most recently, Southwest Detroit General Hospital in 1974, which was a consolidation of four smaller proprietary hospitals in southwest Detroit: Boulevard General, Burton Mercy, Delray General and Trumbull General. These hospitals were small, often former family homes retrofitted to accommodate as many patient beds as possible. Sometimes a four-family flat was reorganized to serve fifteen or twenty patients.

Compared to the large municipal hospitals, the small black proprietary hospitals must have seemed primitive. Detroit physician Dr. Waldo Cain,

67

a graduate of all-black Meharry Medical School in Nashville, recalled the conditions under which doctors at such facilities had to work:

I can recall seeing a patient with intestinal obstruction at old Kirkwood Hospital, and we didn't have a suction machine. Even at Meharry we could hook them up to wall suction. They had these little portable suctions at Kirkwood, but the thing didn't work. It's 3 a.m., and I have this tube down this patient, and the wall suction won't work. They only had one. What I had to do was tell a nursing supervisor to give me an aide and let the aide sit there with a big syringe and just syringe all night long. But it worked. It was the most primitive kind of thing, but they worked. People got well. It took a lot of imagination on the part of the surgeon.[25]

After World War II, the proprietary hospitals began to disappear. Unable to compete with the larger, well-equipped, technology-enhanced public institutions, hospitals like Kirkwood faced increasing scrutiny from accrediting agencies. In the 1960s, federal funding from Medicare and Medicaid imposed stringent standards these institutions could not meet. Southwest Detroit Hospital, the last of such institutions in Detroit, which had cost $21 million to accommodate 246 patient beds, survived for just sixteen years.

Adding to the inadequacy of resources to meet the needs of African Americans, there were too few black physicians to treat too many patients. Many black citizens were already fearful of hospitals based on a longstanding belief that hospital doctors used laboratory tests to conduct experiments on patients. In this era before the development of sulfa drugs, there was also the legitimate and well-documented fear of contracting a serious infection while under a doctor's care in a hospital. As a result, many African Americans in Detroit sought alternative forms of treatment outside the conventional medical establishment.

Alternative health practitioners serving the black community fell into two categories: spiritualists and independent specialists. Spiritualists, or "divine healers," as some preferred to be called, typically offered variations of the tent revival's laying of the hands. Forrester Washington, the first director of the Detroit Urban League, remembered dealing with a particular spiritualist:

One of these healers started in business only a month ago charging 50 cents a treatment. He has built up such a following that he is now charging from $2.00 to $25.00, according to the amount he thinks a patient will be *able to pay. His office is always full of sick blacks who get up early in the morning to be first in line when his place of business opens.*[26]

A secondary category of alternative medicine practitioner was the independent specialist. These herbalists, neighborhood prophets and magic store vendors treated a broad range of physical and mental ailments. Such treatments might have included mystical or religious rituals, the use of roots and herbs and specific directives on what to do or avoid once the patient was home. Not only had the Great Migration brought tens of thousands of blacks from the rural South to work in Detroit's factories, but the diaspora also brought with it a wealth of African folklore, Christian and Vodoun religion, as well as family traditions passed down from one generation to the next, all of which many blacks in Detroit were predisposed to utilize as an antidote to the discriminatory practices they experienced.

Troubled by the poor health of Detroit's black population, the Detroit Urban League launched an observance of National Negro Health Week. Booker T. Washington, founder of the Tuskegee Institute, issued a call for blacks across the nation to join with him in a movement designed to aid in improving health conditions, which he saw as impediments to economic success and, thereby, acceptance into the mainstream of American society. Economic success was seen by Washington as rooted in the pursuits of education, business, property ownership and racial unity.

In 1915, Washington launched the first Health Improvement Week with the cooperation of local organizations and agencies across the country that were in a position to reach and influence the greatest number of African Americans.

In Detroit, under the direction and supervision of John Dancy, the DUL enlisted the aid of physicians to talk to various African American congregations throughout the city on a range of practical health-related topics such as personal hygiene or proper sanitation techniques. In 1919, the DUL established a baby clinic on Columbia Street, staffed by a doctor and three nurses. Five mornings a week, black mothers brought their babies to the clinic, sometimes as many as fifty a day, to be examined and receive clinical instruction on the baby's care and feeding. Many of the mothers had come to Detroit from the rural South and were completely unfamiliar with the state of medical science and had never been attended to by a physician. For many, Dancy concluded, it was eye opening:

Their views, based on their childhood training, clashed with those of the medical profession. Some had been taught that the way to ward off sickness for their children was to hang a bag of asafetida around the child's neck. Another, more modern school of thought held that the best thing to hang around the neck was a dime. It was quite disconcerting to some of the mothers to find that the doctors held even more radical views. "Take the dime off the baby's neck and buy him some milk with it," one doctor said. "It will do him more good."[27]

The baby clinic was such a success that it continued for many years thereafter. The National Negro Health Week lasted until 1951, at which point the U.S. Department of Public Health attempted to integrate community services on the federal level.

PUBLIC ACCOMMODATIONS

A few years after he resigned his position as vice president and general manager of Ford Motor Company, James Couzens considered running for mayor of Detroit. A close associate suggested to him that he consult with John Dancy of the Detroit Urban League for advice on cultivating the black vote. Couzens subsequently planned a dinner party to engage a group of potential donors, including Dancy and a handful of the other influential black community leaders. However, no major downtown Detroit hotel would accommodate such a request, owing to the presence of blacks on the list of guests. Despite his standing within the community, Couzens was hard-pressed to find a venue fitting his needs until, after much negotiation, the YMCA offered to host the event. The Y was largely segregated, and few blacks had been able to use its facilities except through the direct intervention of an important patron. Access to theaters, public parks, hotels, swimming facilities and other accommodations—protected in theory by post–Civil War antidiscrimination laws—was frequently denied or restricted during much of the period of the Great Migration.

Traveling downtown in search of recreation or entertainment for residents of Conant Gardens, Eight Mile–Wyoming or the West Side was problematic. Paradise Valley was not considered a family destination, but it did afford adult access to taverns, dance halls and live entertainment. There was very little for children to do, except go to the Main Public Library on

Original wooden bridge connecting local residents to Detroit's major recreational facility on the Detroit River. *Library of Congress.*

Woodward Avenue and select movie houses, although some offered only balcony seating for blacks. Belle Isle was a popular public venue during the summer months, but on weekends and holidays, blacks and whites competed for baseball diamonds, picnic tables and prime beach spots, causing racial tension and occasional confrontation.

Over the Fourth of July holiday in 1940, a black youth allegedly took a canoe belonging to someone else on Belle Isle. After he returned it under order of a nearby patrolman, the youth ran, was apprehended and was beaten in front of hundreds of black picnickers. The incident further escalated at the police station, where angry protesters who had witnessed the beating scuffled with police. Two protesters were arrested. The black youth, Melvin McConico, was sentenced by a recorder's court judge to thirty days in the House of Corrections; the two protesters were fined and placed on probation.

In 1937, state senator Charles Diggs pushed a bill through Lansing to make it a misdemeanor to deny service based on race, ethnicity or religion. Violators were subject to a twenty-five-dollar fine, fifteen days in jail or

Idyllic waterways on Detroit's recreational gem, Belle Isle. *Library of Congress.*

both. Drugstore lunch counters like Hechtman's and large restaurants like Greenfield's flouted the law and simply paid the fines.[28] In other establishments, denial of service came in many forms—asking black patrons to take their food on paper plates outside to eat, charging higher prices or simply delaying service. This is not to say that there were no restaurants willing to serve African Americans, but certainly for residents of the various black enclaves who were unfamiliar with the lay of the land, a casual visit downtown could turn into a humiliating experience.

And the humiliation was not restricted to downtown venues, as West Eight Mile Road faced its own barriers to recreation. In the 1950s and '60s, the outdoor swimming pool at Joe Louis Park had become the summer locus of recreation for children in the area. Parents were delighted at the time to have such a facility, knowing as they did the very limited access to recreational swimming for blacks in metropolitan Detroit. The Detroit Parks Department managed the Central Community Center on Brewster Street downtown, but it was a long way to travel just to swim.

After the high-rise Brewster Douglass projects were completed, the center admirably served the recreational needs of the more than ten thousand residents of the surrounding high-rises. But it rarely served the needs of the Eight Mile–Wyoming, Conant Gardens or West Side communities, nor was it intended to do so.

The other main option was Belle Isle, even farther south and east, but racial incidents and confrontations had occurred on the island, so West Eight Mile Road and Conant Gardens residents found the journey south not worth the effort. In 1943, such concerns proved justifiable when one incident sparked a race riot with significant loss of life, major injuries and extensive property damage.

African American teenagers living near Eight Mile were hearing on the street about a swimming facility open year-round and just down the road, a five-minute bike ride or ten minutes by foot traveling west along Eight Mile. The place could be the perfect complement, some thought, to the outdoor pool at Joe Louis Park, especially after it shut down at the end of the summer. Located on the northeast corner of Eight Mile and Greenfield Roads, the Crystal Pool was a segregated, membership-only indoor pool with two diving boards and a sixteen-foot diving tower hovering over ten feet of water. At the other end, where the bottom of the pool had sloped upward to create a wading area for smaller children and first-time swimmers—so long as they were white—kids could get acclimated to the water and splash around. A few of the more adventurous black teens in the area had ridden bikes to Greenfield Road and attempted to breach the wall of separation created by the security personnel but had not been successful. Legend has it that a few blacks had in fact been allowed in—or snuck in, depending on what version of the story one heard. The same story had whites either remove themselves from the area where blacks were swimming or confront and harass the black patrons. In either case, it was a place of mystery and ongoing curiosity for local black teens, a place about which parents could never seem to provide an adequate explanation for the stories of rejection.

Segregated pools like the Crystal Pool at the border of Oak Park and Detroit were the byproduct of two basic anxieties felt by whites at the time, according to Jeff Wiltse in *Contested Waters: A Social History of Swimming Pools*. Before the Great Migration, many whites discriminated against first-generation European immigrants based on health concerns rooted in class distinctions. The immigrants were not only filthy and likely disease carriers but also people with whom social—and of course physical—

intercourse was prohibited. After the Great Migration, segregation policies and practices were racialized, and for white supremacists, contamination and miscegenation dovetailed into one fear: close contact with blacks, particularly where black men and white women might share space while wearing provocative clothing, threatened to "infect" the white race.

Frank Joyce, a prominent Detroit New Left civil rights and antiwar activist of the 1960s, recalled the final days of the Crystal Palace, as the owners decided to close its doors rather than integrate the pool:

> *What I trace as my first overt political act was in the summer of 1960. I was driving down the infamous Eight Mile Road, and I happened to notice a picket line, a demonstration that I couldn't really figure out what it was. But I was intrigued by it, so I made a U-turn on Eight Mile Road and I came back, and I saw that it was a protest at a place called the Crystal Palace, and the protest was over the fact that the pool—remember this is 1960 in the North—that Crystal Palace denied admission to African Americans: it was a white-only public swimming pool in Oak Park, Michigan, in 1960. And I said, "Well, that's not right." So, I joined that picket line.*[29]

That night, Joyce's father watched local coverage of the protest on television, saw his teenage son on the picket line and kicked the boy out of the house.

AFRICAN AMERICANS AND WAR HOUSING IN THE SUBURBS

Encircling Detroit were suburban communities with industrial sites that were also receiving defense contracts to produce armaments of war. The Chrysler Tank Plant, the Hudson Naval Ordnance Plant and the Willow Run Bomber Plant all came to life on the outskirts of Detroit. Thousands of defense workers, black and white, migrated to these outlying communities even as infrastructure and public services were ill-prepared to receive them. Of the twenty-eight thousand African Americans who migrated to Wayne County to seek employment in the lead-up to the war, seventeen thousand sought housing in Highland Park and Hamtramck—small cities within Detroit's boundaries—and in the suburban communities of Inkster, River Rouge and Ecorse to be near work and to be as far as possible from the overcrowded, substandard housing on Detroit's near east side.

Nankin Township (today, the city of Westland), for example, was selected by the National Housing Agency as the site for 1,189 single-family homes, duplexes and row houses at a cost of about $12 million. Due to the scarcity of building materials during the war, construction was completed with whatever materials were locally available. It meant, for a time, leaving off trim, gutters and other features normally considered standard in housing construction. Named the Norwayne Subdivision, these modest residences were built on 494 acres roughly bounded by Palmer Road on the north, Wildwood Road on the west, Merriman Road on the east and Glenwood Road and the Wayne County Lower Rouge Parkway on the south.[30]

The original occupancy of this subdivision, the largest public housing project in metro Detroit at the time, was restricted to military personnel and war workers employed at nearby defense industry plants, including the Willow Run Bomber Plant. The subdivision featured two elementary schools—Jefferson-Barns and Lincoln—as well as a community center and various stores.

Construction of Norwayne began in 1942 and was substantially completed by the end of the next year. White defense workers faced little to no waiting time for housing accommodations at Norwayne so long as they met the income criteria, which was $2,000 for a family of two, though the cap was increased by $200 for each child up to four. In fact, by 1944, the subdivision was experiencing only 60 percent occupancy even though the income cap had increased to expand eligibility. At the same time, the Detroit War Housing Center identified over eleven thousand eligible black workers desperately in need of habitable accommodations. Public war housing in suburban Detroit communities where blacks were otherwise welcome—or at least where racially restrictive covenants were not present in land deeds—such as Ecorse, Inkster and Ypsilanti, were at capacity. Ypsilanti, for instance, had a waiting list of two hundred African American families for its one-hundred-unit Park Ridge project. And the list was growing.

Norwayne would illustrate the local and federal failure to exploit underutilized resources at the time of greatest need. It would also justify to any doubters the rationale for the Double V Campaign waged since the outset of the war: that racial equality on the homefront was as much a goal as victory abroad. Though federal officials understood the frustrations expressed by such organizations as the NAACP, they were not going to permit a "test run" of integrated housing at so large and critical a housing project as Norwayne.

No suburban community in southeastern Michigan resisted the "incursion" of blacks into its housing market more than Dearborn. Though twelve to fourteen thousand African Americans commuted to Dearborn every day to work in Ford's factories, they were not welcome to stay after punching out at the time clock. In 1942, Dearborn citizenry elected as mayor Orville Liscus Hubbard, the most outspoken segregationist north of the Mason-Dixon line. For the next thirty-six years, Hubbard—dubbed the "dictator of Dearborn"—would rule with an iron hand, especially as it related to efforts at integration. His campaign to "Keep Dearborn Clean"—a slogan that appeared on the city police cars—was widely understood as code for "Keep Dearborn White." Any suggestion, however, that Hubbard was an outlier in terms of his views on race relations ignored the bigger reality. Hubbard simply gave a face and a voice to widespread views on desegregation from the federal government on down to the typical white property owner in metropolitan Detroit.

In 1944, the Federal Public Housing Authority proposed to Dearborn officials that a 410-unit temporary war housing project for African Americans be built on a vacant parcel of land within the city limits. The Ford Motor Company, through its spokesman, Harry Bennett, maintained a position of neutrality, particularly considering its perceived delicate relationship between city government and its own workforce. Dearborn officials adopted a resolution opposing "Negro housing," but by the time it reached the city council, the language expanded to include all public housing. In 1948, the same year President Truman desegregated the armed forces by Executive Order 9981, Mayor Hubbard organized a campaign to derail a housing project designed to provide more housing for Ford workers. The John Hancock Life Insurance Company was underwriting this housing development, which would cover more than nine hundred acres near Greenfield and Rotunda Drive. Even Henry Ford II endorsed the project, earning the ire of Mayor Hubbard, who had no intention of evolving in his postwar viewpoint on desegregation, even though the Supreme Court had just ruled that racially restrictive covenants were now unenforceable. While a *Dearborn Press* survey the same year suggested that three-quarters of residents were supportive of the project, by November

VENTURING OUTSIDE THE ENCLAVE

when the development was on the ballot for an advisory vote, Hubbard had injected so much racial animus into the public discussion that the results were a foregone conclusion: by a 3–2 vote (15,900 to 10,500), the development was rejected. In 1978, the last year of his administration, only 20 African Americans resided in a city of 90,000.[31]

KEEP THEM CLOSE...BUT NOT TOO CLOSE

Even in the important black enclave of Inkster (important especially to Ford Motor Company), racial segregation was the rule of the day. John Dancy, the charismatic executive director of the Detroit Urban League, had worked with a Mr. Packard, a real estate developer visiting from Florida, to help him locate additional housing for African Americans. The two drove around the city and suburbs, searching for a possible site. Dancy describes the search in his memoirs:

> *We began at Woodward and Seven Mile Road and threaded our way over bad streets and uncharted roads until we had come to 14 Mile Road and Michigan. There, across the railroad tracks at the point that is now Harrison Avenue, we saw a large open space that Mr. Packard decided to buy.*
> *This was March 1921. The property is a part of the city of Inkster. At that time there was not a Negro living within four miles of this area.*[32]

The property alluded to in rural Inkster was 140 acres of undeveloped land in a city without local government or basic public utilities such as streetlights or sewer lines. But it was a place where one could breathe fresh air and begin life anew, away from crowded, unhealthy conditions in Detroit. The property developer would build low-cost cottages for black workers employed at the nearby Ford Rouge complex, with the effect of reinforcing the racial apartheid practiced next door in the city of Dearborn.

As both white and black residents formed the village of Inkster from sections of western Dearborn Township and eastern Nankin Township, a racial division occurred along old township boundaries. School districts reflected this racial division: Nankin No. 7 served the black children, while Dearborn No. 8 served the white children.

By 1930, African Americans made up just over a quarter of the village's 4,440 residents. Over the next decade, as Inkster and the rest of America struggled through the Great Depression, Henry Ford took a special interest in this tiny village that supplied hundreds of workers for his Rouge complex. Ford's rehabilitation program went beyond vague expectations of corporate loyalty; the company's Sociological Department entered the homes of African American Ford employees living in Inkster to determine the worthiness of the applicant for financial assistance. If the domicile was not up to prescribed standards of order and cleanliness, instructions and ultimatums would be given. Proper management of resources—personal loans, material possessions such as an automobile and dietary considerations—would be a major criterion for initial and ongoing participation. A program that had originally begun in Highland Park two decades previous was now restored in Inkster as part of Henry Ford's paternalistic vision.

The Ford "Inkster Project," as it was called, concluded in 1941.

This is all to say that in the summer of 1941, an escalating housing crisis hit the black community in Detroit particularly hard. Promised federal relief, in the form of two hundred permanent war housing units, dedicated exclusively for African American workers in the northeast section of Detroit, was now being threatened by interagency conflict and political meddling. By the time it played out, significant damage was done to the already frayed social fabric of a city at the center of the war effort on the homefront.

3

THE TROUBLE BEGINS

In May 1941, President Roosevelt authorized federal funding for the construction of one thousand dwelling units, two hundred specifically designated for black occupancy. The United States Housing Authority (USHA) authorized the Detroit Housing Commission (DHC) to oversee the building and management of the black housing project. Despite its own preferred site, the DHC deferred to the USHA's decision to locate the project in northeast Detroit, between Conant Gardens, the middle-class black enclave, to the northwest and a large white Polish-Catholic community to the east. Named the Sojourner Truth Homes, the project paid tribute to the abolitionist, author and human rights activist who passed away in Battle Creek, Michigan, in 1888 at the age of eighty-six.

The selection of this site would provoke a dramatic and immediate response from so many constituent groups that the very efficacy of the project came into question. The spark that lit the fuse was a letter written by the Conant Gardens Community Association to Congressman Rudolph Tenerowicz, in whose First District the project was to be located.[33]

The trouble began, it can be said, with a single letter. On June 23, 1941, the Conant Gardens Community Association—ever vigilant to threats concerning property valuations—wrote the following request to Congressman Tenerowicz:

To the Hon. Rudolph G. Tenerowicz,

On behalf of the residents and property owners of the Conant Gardens section of Detroit, I wish to go on record as opposing the building of the proposed defense housing project on the land bounded by Stockton, Fenelon, Nevada, and Justine.

The Conant Gardens section is the approximate area bounded by Seven Mile Road, Ryan, Nevada, and Conant Avenues, and for the past few years has been the scene of much home building and home improvement. This section is the only part of Detroit where the Federal Housing Administration will approve home-construction loans for Negroes. People in this area have built and bought homes ranging in price from $4,000 to $12,000 and are naturally interested in maintaining an atmosphere and environment commensurate with their investment. We feel that the building of the defense homes project in such close proximity to the Conant Gardens section will cause a deterioration in the existing housing values and discourage further building in a section which promises to be a model district and a distinct advantage in a socioeconomic way to the city of Detroit.

We would like to point out another point which causes us to protest the proposed location of this project. The project recreational facilities would of necessity be centered around Pershing High School field and Conant Gardens area lying between the high-school grounds and the proposed project would become a thoroughfare, bringing with it attendant problems.

We are in favor of defense homes but believe that they should be placed where they can help rather than hinder the neighborhood. We hope that you will give this matter your careful consideration and would welcome an opportunity to discuss the matter with you in person.
Awaiting your reply.
CONANT GARDENS COMMUNITY ASSOCIATION
P.S.—You as the Congressman of our district, have always exhibited an understanding of our problems. We urge you to do all in your power to see to it that this project is not built on the proposed site.[34]

Tenerowicz was unaware that a week previous the USHA had rejected the DHC's first choice of sites for defense housing in northeast Detroit. The commission had selected a site for a white project at Mound Road and Outer Drive and a site for an African American project in a predominantly black area at Dequindre and Modern Avenues. On June 16, Earl Von

Storch, USHA construction advisor, formally notified the commission that the white project was being relocated to Centerline, in Macomb County, out of the reach of the DHC. Furthermore, Von Storch indicated that the Dequindre and Modern site, the DHC's first choice for the African American project, would be too inhospitable in that it was located within an industrial site amid factories and railroads. Even the DHC would agree that the site, were it selected for white development, would have been rejected on the face of it. The site would also be expensive to develop, as a railroad spur in the middle of the proposed site would have to be removed and rerouted. On June 19, William K. Divers, USHA director Region V, confirmed the selection of the DHC second choice, a twenty-acre site bounded by Nevada, Fenelon, Stockton and Eureka. Divers further announced that A.F. Harman had been selected as the architect. The USHA had effectively disregarded the DHC's recommendations about both sites and architects.

The Nevada and Fenelon site was a sparsely populated, racially mixed area several miles from the overcrowded and highly segregated Black Bottom and Paradise Valley neighborhoods on the lower east side. The nearby schools—Atkinson Elementary, Cleveland Intermediate School and Pershing High School—had been integrated for years and were within walking distance of the designated defense housing project.

The middle-class black enclave, Conant Gardens, was located immediately to the north and west of the designated site, about four blocks away, while a large Polish community centered on St. Louis the King Parish was located east of Ryan Road. The major objection of the Conant Gardens Community Association to the proposed housing project was socioeconomic; they believed, erroneously, that the project was temporary wartime housing, which, in their estimation, would draw the wrong element to the area—pool halls, beer gardens, after-hours clubs, associated crime and prostitution—and would quickly devalue their property. To persuade the USHA to reconsider their decision, the CGCA believed—also erroneously—that partnering with the Polish neighborhoods to the east would greatly strengthen its hand, as both communities had much to lose economically if the planned housing project were to achieve fruition.

At about the same time Tenerowicz was absorbing the contents of this unexpected letter, members of the CGCA were organizing local residents and planning their next steps. On Tuesday, June 24, 1941, officers of the CGCA distributed circulars door to door announcing a meeting that very night:

There will be a meeting of all residents of the Conant area Tuesday, June 24,
at 8:45 p.m., Pershing High School.
We are meeting to further the protest on the proposed location of homes
for defense workers near Atkinson School.
Time is vital and we must act at once if we are to protect our home
investments.
Come out Tuesday and be on time.[35]

No comparable neighborhood organization east of Ryan Road existed, so members of the CGCA contacted a few white property owners in the nearby Polish community. Word of the meeting spread throughout the day, and by 8:30 p.m. a crowd of more than three hundred descended upon Pershing representing all property interests. Though Mayor Jefferies and each of the housing commissioners were invited to attend, none chose to do so.

Attempts to forge a biracial coalition based on a mutual desire to protect property values slowly degenerated into name-calling. Obvious to several of the Conant Garden residents in attendance was that the white property owners had a different, more virulent reaction to the news of the day. Hostilities between a few blacks and whites in attendance sent others into separate classrooms to try to restore calm and set forward a plan of action that both groups could agree on. One plan that did emerge was to send representatives from the Pershing meeting to meet face to face with Congressman Tenerowicz and representatives of the USHA.

Three days after the events at Pershing High School, Tenerowicz arranged the requested meeting at the offices of F. Charles Starr, regional director No. 5 of the USHA, in Washington, D.C. In attendance were Tenerowicz, Starr, attorney Percival Piper (an assistant to the state attorney general appearing on behalf of the CGCA), two unidentified white property owners from east of Ryan Road and Earl von Storch, construction advisor to the USHA. The ad hoc committee, which brought along petitions signed by approximately 1,400 residents, was uniform in its request to the USHA: find an alternative site for the housing project intended for black defense workers. Starr listened patiently to the committee's arguments and closed the meeting by suggesting that the burden fell on them to locate a more appropriate site and submit a proposal, with all the attendant facts, directly to him.

On July 2, at the prompting of more than three dozen residents in the neighborhood of Fenelon and Nevada, the Detroit City Council wired the USHA requesting it locate the defense housing site elsewhere and reconsider the DHC's original proposed site at Dequindre and Modern. On the advice of Congressman Tenerowicz, Percival Piper wrote to Starr:

Dear Colonel Starr,

This is in line with our recent telegram requesting that the 200-family defense project be located at Dequindre and Modern Streets, in the city of Detroit. This matter was presented to the Common Council of the City of Detroit at its regular meeting on Tuesday, July 1, together with a representative from the Detroit Housing Commission and the Detroit City Planning Commission. After considering same, Council voted to wire you, recommending that the project be located at Dequindre and Modern site.

I am well aware of the conference we had with you and Mr. von Storch when I was in Washington on June 27, but since my return to the city I have had a number of persons to get in touch with me who do not live in the vicinity of Nevada and Fenelon, but who concur that it would certainly be unharmonious to erect a defense housing project on that site and they believe that the Dequindre-Modern site would be appropriate. There is a spur railroad track which, we believe, could be moved and the project would then not be sitting directly on the belt line. The Nevada property is across the street from manufacturing and industrial concerns and the belt railroad tracks.

I was looking at another site at the intersection of East Davison and Oakland Avenues which covers a large amount of territory, on the northeast corner, and it may be that some consideration may be given to that site.

Again thanking you for your kind consideration to our committee when in Washington and hoping that you will accept the wishes of the vast majority of the home owners in the Ryan-Fenelon district, and that you will change the location from that district and use the one at Dequindre and Modern.

Sincerely,
Percival Piper[36]

Hoping to muster support from even more powerful and politically connected allies and reduce the burden on his shoulders as a relatively new congressman, Tenerowicz pressed Piper to pen yet another letter, this time to Democratic senator Prentiss Brown, who had been selected five years before to replace the deceased senator from Michigan, James Couzens. That letter, dated July 8, offered a lengthy analysis of why the defense homes should not be built at Fenelon and Nevada, including such interesting arguments as "It is believed that it will cause a number of owners to become delinquent with Federal Housing Administration mortgages and other contract payments if this project is erected on Nevada Street." Once Conant Garden residents learned from the USHA that the defense project was to be permanent housing, their immediate fears dissipated, but deeper regrets surfaced as it became obvious that the meeting to create a biracial coalition had, in fact, driven a deeper wedge between the communities. Property owners in Conant Gardens now saw white resistance to the housing project in a new light: what they thought would be a shared socioeconomic concern was now deeply racial.

The miscalculation by the CGCA in calling the biracial meeting at Pershing High School had profound consequences that would be deeply regretted by residents for years to come. The meeting had stirred the pot, and now the pot was about to boil over. The degree of racial animosity within and between various factions in the city of Detroit spilled over into the national consciousness and would have repercussions in other communities struggling with housing issues across the country.

THE SEVEN MILE–FENELON HOMEOWNERS IMPROVEMENT ASSOCIATION (SMFHIA)

An immediate consequence of the Pershing High School meeting was the galvanization of various white interests in torpedoing the black defense housing project. The "spontaneous" creation of the Seven Mile–Fenelon Homeowners Improvement Association had little to do with addressing residential structures, habitation and commercial properties. Its boilerplate bylaws and regulations were merely a cover for its sole obsession: to enlist as many local white residents and organizational entities as "soldiers" in the army fighting federal interference in a local matter. The DHC had, in fact, already located the project at another site—albeit one that needed improvement at some expense to make it habitable. The federal government, and all its various agencies and representatives, had erred grievously, and it would now need to acknowledge the error, correct it and move on. There was an overseas war to be fought, after all. It was almost a matter of Christian faith that this new association was fighting the good fight.

It was fitting that the Seven Mile–Fenelon Homeowners Improvement Association (SMFHIA) conducted its meetings at St. Louis the King

Bishop Galagher presiding over the 1924 dedication of St. Louis the King Polish Catholic Church, Detroit, Michigan. Assisting the bishop are brothers Alexander and Bernard Jarzembowski, both diocesan priests in the Archdiocese of Detroit. *Author's collection.*

St. Louis the King Church, located at 18891 St. Louis Avenue, Detroit, Michigan. *Author's collection.*

Parish Church, pastored by the Reverend Constantine Dzink. Although the SMFHIA was headquartered in a storefront at 19235 Fenelon, its spiritual and moral compass was in the center of the Polish Catholic community at a church presided over by an unabashedly racist and anti-Semitic cleric. Father Dzink was much beloved by his parishioners, and he had no difficulty exerting the spiritual and moral authority that would make their blind participation in protesting the black housing project a given. Once he got his congregation fully on board with resistance to the housing project, he would turn his attention to the USHA. In a letter to Michigander Charles F. Palmer, national director of the USHA in Washington, Father Dzink gave a toned-down version of his normally vitriolic rhetoric:

Dear Mr. Palmer,

The USHA is considering the construction of a low-cost housing project in the vicinity of Fenelon and Nevada Streets for the colored people.

This, my dear Mr. Palmer, would mean utter ruin for many people who have mortgaged their homes to the FHA and not only that, but it would jeopardize the safety of many of our white girls, as no colored people live closely by. Lastly, it would ruin the neighborhood, one that could be built up into a fine residential section.

It is the sentiment of all people residing within the vicinity to object against this project in order to stop race riots in the future. Can we then appeal to your sense of fair play, and with your final decision feel that you will prove a friend of ours, now that we are helpless and seek a friend to override this project.

May I feel that I have found a friend in you, Mr. Palmer, and that the many sleepless nights that I have spent in trying to ward off this future danger to my parish and its citizens will not prove in vain, but your sound judgement in this matter will be a fond memory of calling to mind a true and honest friend. With all confidence that you will decide in our favor against the project, I beg to remain,
Yours sincerely,
Rev. C. Dzink
Pastor[37]

Dzink's reference to the project jeopardizing "the safety of many of our white girls" would be one of several despicable themes repeated not only in his Sunday sermons but also carried over into the various outgoing communications of the SMFHIA.

Politically, local realtor Joseph P. Buffa, who owned as many as one thousand lots throughout the area, led the association as its first president and directed a campaign of letter writing, telephone calling, visiting local politicians, creating placards and posters and picketing diverse venues. Other officers within the association were local Polish Catholics who, while working factory shifts, could count on spouses to function as surrogates if marching or picketing or making calls were required by Buffa or his associates.

THE ORIGINS OF THE PROBLEM

Father Dzink and his St. Louis the King parishioners, as well as Joseph Buffa and his real estate associates, felt a legitimate sense of betrayal. From the federal government down to municipal authorities, public housing policy and practice had been consistently discriminatory against African Americans. Why the change now? Here?

The explanation requires revisiting 1933, the year of an important policy initiative formulated at the outset of the Roosevelt administration. To simultaneously jumpstart the construction industry while addressing the critical housing shortage, Roosevelt created the Public Works Administration (PWA), which would develop and implement a public housing program. Newly appointed Secretary of the Interior Harold Ickes, a noted liberal on matters of race, assumed the helm of the construction program. Former president of the Chicago branch of the NAACP, Ickes was acutely aware of how severely the housing shortage affected African Americans throughout the country. Despite a measure of resistance from other administration officials who had envisioned public housing as serving middle- and working-class white families exclusively, Ickes designated nearly one-third of new housing units for black occupancy.

Unwilling or unable to affect a policy of integrated housing, Ickes established a neighborhood composition rule, in which any new housing project should reflect the racial composition of the previous neighborhood. Thus, a new project in a previously black neighborhood would be a segregated black project; a new project in a previously white neighborhood would remain exclusively white. And in theory, a new project in a mixed area would allow for mixed occupancy. However, in practice, the PWA would designate a mixed area as either black or white and build a project exclusively white or black, obliterating the mixed nature of the original community.

In 1937, Congress terminated the PWA's program of directly funding construction of local housing projects. In its place, localities had the option of creating their own housing authorities and seeking construction subsidies from the newly created United States Housing Authority. The USHA had every intention of maintaining the neighborhood composition rule and continued the practice of segregating even integrated communities.

A few years later, the winds of war were blowing across the Atlantic, and Congress enacted the Lanham Act, which would be the legal mechanism to provide financing for workers in defense industries. Also, in 1940, the newly created Division of Defense Housing (DDH), a part of the PWA, would develop and manage the housing of war industry workers. Clark Foreman, a friend and protégé of Harold Ickes, was appointed director of the DDH, and late the following year, he became a pivotal figure in the Sojourner Truth housing controversy. As Richard Rothstein concludes in *The Color of Law* (2017), "By the war's end, the Lanham Act had combined with PWA and USHA programs to create or solidify racial segregation in every metropolitan area they had touched."[38]

Detroit was ahead of the curve among major metropolitan areas by establishing a housing commission in 1933 under the Michigan Housing Facilities Act and funded by a grant from the Federal Emergency Housing Corporation. Josephine Gomon, the DHC's first and a widely respected director, was both a visionary and realist at the same time. It became obvious to her early on that integrated public housing would be a tough sell in Detroit. The PWA had designed and funded the development of Detroit's first public housing projects: Parkside Homes for whites and Brewster Homes for blacks. Eleanor Roosevelt was so interested in the Brewster Homes project that she attended the groundbreaking in 1935. In 1938, the PWA turned over management of the two projects to the DHC. A public debate over the efficacy of public housing—even segregated public housing—played out in the local newspapers, and editorial pages were filled with contrarian points of view. Members of the Common Council were divided on the issue, but there was no division within the Wider Woodward Association, a group of white business owners located on the city's main thoroughfare, who were adamant that any public housing in Detroit keep the races segregated. Gomon was able to mitigate the damage of any criticism coming her way concerning the establishment of public

THE TROUBLE BEGINS

housing in Detroit, regardless of racial occupancy, by personal diplomacy and moderation in her pronouncements. She made many friends—and very few enemies—among Detroit's varied racial and ethnic groups in Detroit during the period of her brief two-year tenure. No one who succeeded her, certainly during the war years, was able exert the influence and generate the goodwill of Josephine Gomon.[39]

At Brewster Homes, George A. Isabel was named resident manager (Eugene P. Opperman, at Parkside). Selecting tenants from among the numerous applicants was the first order of the day, and that process began in earnest during the summer of 1938. The number of applications for Brewster swelled to 6,059—for Parkside, 5,951. The process took nearly six months because of having to satisfy each tenant's eligibility requirements, which were somewhat reminiscent of the intrusive employment hiring measures employed by Ford Motor Company's Sociological Department in the 1920s (and more recently revived in Ypsilanti). Detroit public housing applicants had to demonstrate that at least one family member living in the projects was employed full time, that income limits not be exceeded and that the applicant submit to an inspection of their current living conditions, from which the overall "fitness" of the prospective tenant be ascertained. To a large degree, the fitness issue gave the resident manager the greatest degree of latitude—and the greatest possibility for abuse—in determining who obtained a coveted housing unit. Considering the conditions in which so many of the Black Bottom applicants were consigned to live, most often in overcrowded, decrepit hovels, it's a wonder anyone qualified as fit applicants.

By 1942, the die was cast, and any attempts at social engineering by integrating public housing was lost with these first federally funded low-rise housing projects in Detroit. Harold Ickes's neighborhood composition rule had been realized in practice, not merely in principle, and this new federal policy of racial segregation in federally funded projects would transfer over to federally funded wartime housing.

A BUILDING STORM OF PROTEST IN NORTHEAST DETROIT

In some respects, the property at Nevada and Fenelon was a choice between two evils. The Detroit Housing Commission had assumed that the Division of Defense Housing would accept the DHC's first choice of building sites, the industrial site located at the intersection of Dequindre and Modern. Rejected on the grounds that the site was inhospitable for housing and too expensive to develop, federal officials chose the DHC's second choice. Neither the DDH nor the DHC had performed its due diligence with respect to the secondary site option. In "Homes for Defense," a document issued by the DDH, the method for selecting a defense housing project is laid out in general terms:

> *Before formulating a specific program for a defense area several preliminary steps are necessary, of which the foremost is a thoughtful and thorough examination of the community problem. Such examination aids materially in preventing dislocation of the normal life of the community, which is a vitally necessary consideration.*[40]

This is not to say that Detroit's Housing Commission did not review a range of possible sites for the proposed black housing project. Given the already overcrowded and highly segregated state of the city, anyone would have been hard-pressed to locate an ideal site. As Clark Foreman, director of the DDH, pointed out in congressional testimony, "The site for additional black housing would inevitably be an area where blacks did not already live."

So, neither the Dequindre/Modern nor the Nevada/Fenelon site would be considered ideal, though for completely different reasons. The DDH, however, continued to press on and keep the construction plans on schedule, despite intensifying opposition by Congressman Tenerowicz, the newly formed Seven Mile–Fenelon Homeowners Improvement Association and Father Dzink and his parishioners at St. Louis the King Parish, as well as real estate interests in the area.

Meanwhile, the Conant Gardens Community Association had withdrawn its opposition to the housing project, having recently learned that it was to be a permanent settlement, not the cheaply constructed temporary "barracks" that residents had believed. More importantly, perhaps, residents had become alarmed at the blatant racial tone of the protest emanating from the Polish parish. The association's intent to join with the whites in the area had been based on what they perceived to be a shared belief that property values would be threatened by such a project, not out of any racial animus. To learn that the argument advanced by white homeowners and local parishioners was less about socioeconomics and more about race was both bewildering and humiliating. In the days

I SELL THE SHADOW TO SUPPORT THE SUBSTANCE.

SOJOURNER TRUTH.

Portrait of Sojourner Truth, the civil rights and women's rights activist, after whom the controversial Detroit war housing project was named. *Library of Congress.*

and weeks ahead, many of the association members would feel a profound sense of guilt over what they had initiated by seeking to meet jointly with their white neighbors in a common cause.

President Roosevelt did not like to place too much authority in the hands of any one individual or agency and divided up responsibilities for housing under various agencies. At any given point, one agency—the PWA, the USHA or the DDH, for example—would participate in the decision-making regarding housing, whether it be public housing or housing designated specifically for war industry workers. For example, on September 4, the USHA, not the DDH, negotiated a $849,900 construction contract with a Lansing firm after twice failing to obtain competitive construction bids. Despite the objection of the DHC to this negotiation, it agreed as agent on behalf of the USHA to approve the final contract.

With construction now planned and a builder assigned—and possibly to salve inter-agency wounds—federal officials within the USHA invited the DHC to officially name the new housing development at Fenelon and Nevada. The DHC deferred to the Reverend Horace A. White, the commission's lone black member. When White chose to honor the former slave and civil rights activist Sojourner Truth by naming the project after her, the other commissioners—Donald Sabbe, Ethan Thompson, Harriet Kelly and Edward Thal—voted unanimously to accept this recommendation and notified the USHA of this choice on September 29. By so doing, the DHC seemed to signal its acceptance of the project as a future African American settlement.

WHO WAS SOJOURNER TRUTH?

Sojourner Truth (born Isabella Baumfree) was a nineteenth-century evangelist, abolitionist and civil and women's rights activist. Born into slavery in Swartekill, New York, in 1797, she was sold four times before the age of twenty-six. When her final owner reneged on a promise to emancipate her in 1826, she fled with her daughter Sophia, the youngest of five children, to the home of an abolitionist family, the Van Wageners. The family bought her freedom for twenty dollars and helped her relocate to New York City with two of her children, following the rare instance of a black woman successfully suing a white man who had illegally sold her young son into slavery.

Once in New York City, she worked as a domestic for a local preacher and developed into a charismatic speaker during the Second Great Awakening, a Protestant religious revival that continued into the mid-1830s. In 1843, she renamed herself Sojourner Truth, declaring that the Spirit called her to preach the truth. She subsequently joined the Northampton Association in Florence, Massachusetts, a utopian community dedicated to justice and equality. There and in her travels as an itinerant preacher, Truth exchanged viewpoints with such influential abolitionists as Frederick Douglass, Wendell Phillips, William Lloyd Garrison and David Ruggles.

Unable to read or write, Truth dictated her autobiography to a close associate who arranged for its publication. The book helped garner her a substantial national reputation and considerably stabilized her finances. During this time, she was befriended by other women's rights advocates, particularly by Susan B. Anthony and Elizabeth Cady Stanton. A year later, she began a lecture tour that eventually took her to a women's rights conference in Akron, Ohio, where she delivered her most famous speech, "Ain't I a Woman?" The speech highlighted the flaws associated with racial and gender stereotypes.

Later, she moved to be with her three daughters in Battle Creek, Michigan, but remained active in various causes, including encouraging young black men to join the Union army at the outset of the Civil War. Toward the end of the war, she spent time in Washington, D.C., helping to desegregate the city's streetcars and addressing a range of national issues. Before she concluded her stay, she was warmly received at the White House by President Abraham Lincoln.

Having retired from public life in 1875, she remained in Battle Creek with her daughters until her death in November 1883.

QUIET BEFORE THE STORM

Throughout October, building at the Nevada and Fenelon site continued without interruption. Foundations for all the buildings had been poured, and the project manager from Lansing responsible for the pace of construction wanted to get as much of the framing and exterior work done before winter set in. On Halloween, which fell on a Friday, the Detroit Housing Commission began taking registrations from African American defense workers for the new housing units and would continue to do so the following Monday and for several days thereafter.

Behind the scenes, Congressman Tenerowicz, members of the SMFHIA—particularly realtors Joseph Buffa and John Dalzell—and representatives from St. Louis the King Parish met weekly to plan a series of disruptive activities that would cast doubt on the fairness of the decision-making process and raise concerns about the social and economic impact of African Americans moving into the soon-to-be-completed defense housing project. Picket lines at city hall were organized, most often with the women of St. Louis the King, sometimes pushing baby carriages, while their husbands were pulling shifts at the nearby factories. In addition, Buffa and Dalzell seized every opportunity to speak at DHC and city council meetings. A vigorous letter-writing campaign, directed at local and federal agency officials, began in earnest. Tenerowicz believed that local and federal officials were sincerely listening to the various objections raised by himself and his northeast Detroit constituents. Talking to the right people at all levels of government, from Mayor Jeffries and city councilmen and housing commissioners all the way up to the various federal agency officials, would, he believed, pay dividends if they continued to apply consistent pressure.

Federal officials from the various overlapping agencies did little to directly discourage Tenerowicz or his associates. Perhaps they believed that keeping detractors at bay just long enough until black residents began to settle into Sojourner Truth Homes would defuse the situation. Telling them "No" too soon risked organized resistance and rebellion. Colonel Starr, USHA regional director, in response to a letter from a local resident inquiring about the status of the project, sent copies of his response to several of the writer's neighbors. He insisted that nothing had been or would be decided regarding occupancy with respect to race. Part of the letter, dated November 8, reads:

> *I have very little to add to our past correspondence on this subject but should like to bring to your attention the results of conferences held in Washington on August 18 and 19 last between representatives of the Federal Works Agency and the United States Housing Authority.*
>
> *At that time, it was agreed that the development of the project would proceed as planned, but that the question of racial occupancy would remain open until construction was completed and tenant selection started, at which time the matter would be settled.*
>
> *No further action has been taken, and the matter rests as it was left then.*[41]

Even Clark Foreman, DDH director, perhaps the most liberal administration official and certainly the staunchest supporter of black occupancy of the Sojourner Truth Homes, followed the same strategy. One month later, on December 9, Foreman replied to a letter from Joseph Buffa, president of the SMFHIA, reassuring him in a similar vein:

> *This will acknowledge your letter of December 1, containing protest against the housing project at Nevada and Fenelon Avenues, Detroit, Mich.*
> *The question of the occupancy of that project is still being studied, and before any final decision is made, your protest will be given every consideration.*[42]

Meanwhile, local officials were becoming alarmed that organized resistance to black occupancy was having an effect in unexpected ways. Buffa and his associates, using the levers of power in Congressman Tenerowicz's Washington office, found allies within the FHA. The agency notified Clark Foreman of the DDC that if blacks were to occupy the Sojourner Truth Homes, federally insured loans in the area would be suspended, thus putting in jeopardy the kind of construction loans needed to further develop the surrounding neighborhoods in the future.

On November 17, the DHC authorized Reverend White to confer on the matter of black occupancy directly with Congressman Tenerowicz and USHA officials and, hopefully, put an end to the controversy. Quite the opposite occurred, however, as Reverend White expressed alarm upon his return at both the strident tone of Tenerowicz's voice and the implication of what he was now proposing to take place. The congressman wanted a new land survey and a public hearing to discuss the findings.

Reverend White suddenly became a vocal critic of the congressman, fearing that the resistance movement was moving in a dangerous direction. A public hearing, at this stage of the construction process, would provide a platform for the kind of inflammatory rhetoric that Joseph Buffa was now spewing at every opportunity. The use of such words as *rioting* and *bloodshed*, as well as racially derogatory terms, was heard increasingly at resistance rallies around St. Louis the King Parish, and Buffa's unruly supporters were becoming even more aggressive.

Louis Murphy and Marie Conti of the *Catholic Worker* newspaper paid a visit to St. Louis the King to interview parishioners concerning the Sojourner Truth controversy. Troubled by all the flag waving by Catholics assigned to man the various picket lines and the message such symbolism was invoking, the pair of interviewers tried to approach various members from a religious rather than political perspective. In one rather galling exchange with a parishioner, Conti recalled, "I said to a Catholic, self-called, that Christ died for both white and Negro—and he actually denied it." Another "good Catholic" accused members of the Catholic Workers movement of not being "real" Catholics, but communists and "n—— lovers." At this point, Murphy and Conti decided to step away and reconsider how to strategically re-engage with the parish members. Unfortunately, their plans were terminated when they were followed by a group of men making menacing gestures and uttering threats. Conti concluded, "I have never in my life seen hate personified as I did in the persons of those Catholics."[43]

AS WINTER APPROACHES…THINGS HEAT UP

Congressman Tenerowicz was beginning to understand that one of the biggest obstacles to a favorable resolution (for his Polish constituents) was Clark Foreman himself. Foreman, the liberal protégé of Secretary of the Interior Harold Ickes, had made several enemies during his ascent to the directorship of the Division of Defense Housing. Tenerowicz learned that there was no love lost between Foreman and Congressman Frank Boykin of Alabama, ranking Democrat on the Committee on Public Buildings and Grounds.

Years earlier, Lyndon B. Johnson, congressman from Texas, recommended Foreman as head of the PWA's Power Division. During his tenure, Foreman crossed paths with Boykin, whose professional career depended on preserving the private corporate interests of Alabama Power. Foreman's agency intended to create a federally owned corporation, the Tennessee Valley Authority, which would provide much cheaper electricity to inhabitants of Tennessee, Alabama, Mississippi, Georgia, North Carolina and Virginia. It was—and remains—the largest regional planning agency of the federal government. Alabama's loss in federal court to Foreman's Power Division left Boykin resenting Foreman. However, it apparently was even more personal than losing a political battle. Some years later, Boykin had asked Foreman to appoint his brother as project manager for a new housing project near Mobile. After carefully reviewing the man's credentials, Foreman concluded he was poorly prepared for such a project and rejected his application.

Boykin never forgot, and now he had an opportunity to settle scores when Tenerowicz came calling.[44]

On January 3, Foreman wired the DHC to proceed with occupancy. Under the Lanham Act, the Committee on Public Buildings and Grounds processed housing appropriations bills for the Division of Defense Housing. In this instance, Tenerowicz had little difficulty persuading Boykin to hold up funds until such time as the PWA asked for Foreman's resignation. Tenerowicz purportedly made it clear to public officials at the PWA that "no money would be released unless that n—— lover [Foreman] was fired and the project returned to white occupancy." The PWA capitulated and asked for his resignation. On January 5, Foreman wired the DHC directing the commission to disregard his previous wire.

With Foreman now out of the picture, Tenerowicz could focus attention on persuading Charles F. Palmer, DDH coordinator directly over the aforementioned Foreman; Baird Snyder III, newly appointed FWA administrator; and Charles Edgecomb, who had just become director-secretary of the Detroit Housing Commission. Edgecomb had brought to the DHC a reputation for being unsympathetic to assertive blacks and white liberals. On January 15, Tenerowicz arranged for a meeting of several federal officials, including Palmer and Snyder, and two local officials, Edgecomb and Reverend White.

The meeting involved a tense exchange between Tenerowicz and White, with the congressman railing against the basic unfairness of the site selection process and suggesting a distinct possibility of rioting if blacks were to assume residency. When White took the bait and stated that violence would be met with violence, the federal officials present concluded that the only workable solution was to re-assign Nevada and Fenelon to the growing list of white defense housing projects. Sojourner Truth's name was taken off the project. To appease black interests, an alternate site would be found immediately, presumably the one originally proposed by the DHC.

To justify the about-face, Tenerowicz and others would cite the formal policy of the DDH regarding sites for defense housing for black occupancy:

It should be the basic policy of the Federal agency selecting sites for defense housing to secure the opinions, approval, and cooperation of the local housing authorities and/or other responsible public and civic groups, including responsible Negro leadership, before a final decision and public announcement is made of a site. This should tend to offset possible local opposition.[45]

The problem with the policy was not its clarity or logic, but its timeliness. The policy was published on January 28, eleven days after the Sojourner Truth housing project had been reassigned. Nonetheless, Tenerowicz could return home to his Polish constituents, particularly at St. Louis the King Parish, with a sense of triumph.

4

PUNCH...COUNTERPUNCH

W hat had begun as a "neighborhood squabble," in the words of *Detroit News* editor Martin S. Hayden, "grew quickly into a city-wide racial dispute [and] has now become magnified into what some regard as one of the nation's primary problems of war-time unity." Undermining the nation's perceived role as champion of democracies and democratic institutions were federal policies and practices that would deny African Americans equal justice under the law. No less a figure than Eleanor Roosevelt would opine to readers of the *Negro Digest*, "If I were a Negro today, I think I would have moments of great bitterness. It would be hard for me to sustain my faith in democracy or to build up a sense of goodwill toward men of other races."[46]

THE BREADTH AND DEPTH OF THE REACTION

On January 22, the Detroit Housing Commission wired the Department of Defense Housing seeking a definite commitment to a black defense housing project. The very same day, DDH officials wired that three hundred homes for black defense workers would be built at the Dequindre and Modern site and that land acquisition would begin immediately. Just four days later, however, on January 26, field agents for the USHA reported that the Ford Motor Company had purchased the site for a new war production plant and that there were no more suitable sites within existing African American neighborhoods. The agents recommended that a site be found outside city limits. The neighborhood composition rule, established by the FWA in 1933, had come home to roost.

Meanwhile, Mayor Jeffries argued before Common Council that the city should go on record for "Negro" occupancy. He took this step, subsequently approved by a majority of councilmen, when faced with the choice of doing so in this manner or ordering the project moved outside the city. "That," Jeffries told the council, "would be tantamount to saying to the Negroes that there is no place within Detroit where they can have new housing. It strikes me that this matter has degenerated into a question of whether government can formally declare itself as favoring racial discrimination. Such a statement would be far different than an individual declaration and I do not believe that, in a democracy, a government can so put itself on record."[47]

Mayor Jeffries was hardly alone in his frustration with political meddling and federal flip-flopping at a time when the entire country needed to remain focused and unified. A local controversy was now gaining traction as a regional and national issue, and powerful voices within and outside the city of Detroit were about to be heard.

If Jeffries and a council majority felt a moral obligation to take a stand in favor of black occupancy, leading African Americans in Detroit took the obligation a significant step further. The Reverend Horace White, who had attended the January 15 meeting in Washington and was the special target of Congressman Tenerowicz's vitriol, wasted no time in contacting the influential state senator Charles C. Diggs, who knew exactly how to translate moral outrage into bold action. It was imperative, Diggs believed, that action take place promptly while the situation in Washington was fluid. Waiting for the ink to dry on these federal proclamations would be deadly to the present cause.

Diggs immediately assembled a group of Detroit's most prominent black citizens, not armchair intellectuals but movers and shakers within the black community; they included Louis Martin, first editor of the *Michigan Chronicle*, the state's largest black newspaper; Dr. James J. McClendon, president of the Detroit Branch of the NAACP; Percival Piper, an assistant to the state attorney general who had been so helpful earlier to local residents of Conant Gardens; the Reverend Charles A. Hill, the popular pastor of Hartford Avenue Baptist Church; Lebron Simmons, an young attorney and an activist within the National Negro Congress; and others. The first meeting, held informally at the St. Antoine branch of the YMCA on the lower east side of

Detroit, provided the necessary focus and resolve to kickstart the resistance. Without dissent, the Reverend Hill was elected chairman, with Lebron Simmons serving as treasurer.

The African American churches of Detroit, in all their various forms and denominations, were a perpetual source of spiritual nourishment and moral guidance for the city's struggling minority. In late January, this small coterie of black leaders organized the Sojourner Truth Citizens Committee (STCC) under the auspices of various black churches to raise money, preach social justice, distribute leaflets and newsletters and encourage individuals to man picket lines, write letters, send telegrams and communicate with public officials face-to-face as the opportunities arose.

These church meetings served as the perfect counterpoint to the meetings that were held at St. Louis the King Parish, not to mention the thirty-five other Polish parishes around the city whose pastors, in most instances, lent quiet support for white occupancy of the new housing project. This is not to say there were no liberal Catholics supportive of black occupancy, but they were neither organized nor outspoken. With respect to Catholic Church hierarchy, the higher one moved up the ecclesiastical chain, the more reserved or muted the response with respect to the housing crisis. At the very top, within the chancery, not a single public utterance was forthcoming from Archbishop Edward J. Mooney.

Within the Jewish community, there were mixed levels of support. Several individuals and organizations provided financial support but were reluctant to participate more openly, fearing an anti-Semitic backlash. Sam Lieberman, longtime leader of the East Side Merchants Association, for instance, provided a great deal of financial support directly to the STCC. Others, like Jack Raskin, a member of the newly formed STCC, used the offices of the Civil Rights Federation, which he headed, to encourage various Jewish community leaders to publicly support black occupancy of the Sojourner Truth Homes. Some individuals, however, were nervous about aligning themselves with the federation ever since it had drawn the attention of the FBI for its association with the communist left. Nevertheless, several rabbis and other prominent Jews officially and publicly added their names to the list of supporters of black occupancy, including Rabbi Leon Fram, Temple Israel; Rabbi Dr. Leo M. Franklin, rabbi emeritus, Temple Beth El; Ernest Goodman, attorney; and Herman Jacobs, director, Jewish Community Center.[48]

From among the city's white churches and clergy, the Reverend Henry Hitt Crane, pastor of Central Methodist Church, emerged as a powerful advocate of interracial cooperation and support for the Sojourner Truth project. Crane's church sermons and public pronouncements were especially noteworthy because of his well-deserved reputation for persuasive oratory and the historic prominence of Central Methodist Church. Within days of the DDH announcement of the change in occupancy, Crane formed an eight-member Action Committee of the Interracial Commission, drawing the immediate support and participation of the Reverend Hill. Both would work closely together in opposition of the federal action and sponsor interracial meetings to keep both white and black communities up-to-date on the issue. Crane was not without community detractors, particularly other white pastors who believed that Crane had put them in an impossible situation, pitting black against white. Crane received a few scolding letters, including some directly opposing black occupancy using the same arguments put forth by Father Dzink and the SMFHIA.[49]

By the time the STCC next met, just two days after its initial organizational meeting at the YMCA, a considerable groundswell of support had been generated by the expanding network established by church leaders, public officials and community activists. The newly minted chairman of the STCC initially saw the controversy as an opportunity to plead with the Polish Americans who fought against black occupancy for working-class solidarity. In an open letter to the Polish community living in the vicinity of Sojourner Truth, Reverend Hill wrote that blacks and Poles were "in the same boat together," as both had been historically vilified. Reverend Hill went on to enumerate the kinds of harmful stereotypes to which both groups had fallen victim. Ultimately, Hill would conclude that his efforts to bridge the divide had been for naught.

This second meeting of the STCC, held at 3:00 p.m. on January 23 at Calvary Baptist Church on Clinton Avenue, drew a crowd of three hundred community members, anxious to move forward with an agenda that would, at this point, be short on words and long on action. Everyone seemed to understand what was at stake beyond local defense housing; the struggle now, here, was for racial justice. There was a general sense that lawmakers in Washington were listening and nervously watching what was happening in Detroit. And if they were not, they soon would. In many instances, members in attendance were representatives of various black and biracial organizations, such as the Michigan Civil Rights Federation, the UAW (particularly Ford Local 600), the Detroit and Wayne County AFL, the CIO, Detroit Youth Assembly and as many as three dozen other organizations and church groups. Immediately after the meeting, the Reverend Hill sent off a sharply worded telegram to President Roosevelt, the first lady, Governor Murray Van Wagoner, Mayor Jeffries, city councilmen, select members of the state legislature and various federal officials. It reminded the recipients that wartime was no time to raise "the color issue in the arsenal of democracy and rob Negro defense workers of the Sojourner Truth Homes built by the Federal Government."

First Lady Eleanor Roosevelt, an ardent integrationist and strong supporter of defense housing for African Americans in general and for black occupancy specifically at Sojourner Truth, received fourteen telegrams urging a reversal of the January 15 decision, one of which was from the Reverend Hill. Because of her presence at the groundbreaking and dedication of the Brewster Homes earlier in the decade, it was believed she would make the case on their behalf directly with the president. It was also believed that Mary McLeod Bethune, a close friend of the first lady, would exert additional pressure within the White House, to which she had unparalleled access, particularly considering she was a black female professional, not a domestic turning beds or preparing meals. Bethune was president of Bethune-Cookman College, a private historically black university in Daytona Beach, Florida.

Mary McLeod Bethune was also a member of the informally named "Black Cabinet," or "Black Cabineteers," a group of forty-five black community leaders holding positions as advisors on matters of civil rights within numerous executive agencies in Washington, D.C. Many of these Cabineteers were acutely aware of events unfolding in Detroit and were exerting what influence they had within their various departments or agencies to resolve this issue favorably. These members included Ralph Bunche, a native Detroiter and an analyst in the Office of Strategic Management; William H. Hastie, a Harvard-educated assistant solicitor for the Department of the Interior; Eugene K. Jones, executive secretary of the National Urban League, serving during the war as advisor on Negro affairs within the Department of Commerce; Lawrence A. Oxley, who had entered government service as director of the Division of Negro Relief for North Carolina, under the Federal Emergency Relief Administration, and was serving in a variety of roles within the Department of Labor, most notably as conciliator in industrial labor disputes; and Robert C. Weaver, trained as an economist, advisor on racial problems in the Department of the Interior and later to become the first African American member of the federal cabinet as secretary of housing and urban development. Bunche would eventually receive the Nobel Peace Prize for his work as United Nations mediator in Palestine, securing the necessary signatures on the armistice agreement

African Americans peaceably assemble in Cadillac Square in downtown Detroit to protest the decision by the federal government to reverse its original stance and declare the Sojourner Truth housing project a white settlement. *Walter P. Reuther Library, Archives of Labor and Urban Affairs, Wayne State University.*

between Israel and the Arab States in 1949. Hastie would become the first African American federal judge, appointed by Roosevelt to the District Court of the Virgin Islands. If nothing else, members of the Black Cabinet made sure the sensitive issue of racial justice would be kept on the front burner in Washington and that any efforts at discrimination would not be countenanced.[50]

In Detroit, more than three thousand individuals supportive of black occupancy were now attending meetings held at local churches, volunteering to distribute literature containing the latest updates and seeking additional volunteers. Many participated in regular picket duty around city hall; others agreed to join a large group of picketers at the meeting of the Detroit Housing Commission on Monday, January 26, at 4:00 p.m. in the Water Board Building on Jefferson Avenue. Maximum pressure was being exerted at all levels of decision-making in Detroit and in the nation's capital. There was an increasing sense of unity and cohesiveness among participants as many came to realize for the first time what was at stake for African Americans.

Wishing to resolve the issue, once and for all, leaders of the STCC were convinced that it was time to pull its most powerful card: sending a large delegation to Washington to obtain an audience with the president. Absent that meeting, other powerful decision-makers would be targeted. Presidential aide Marvin McIntyre, who received word of the plans to send a substantial delegation to the capital, immediately consulted with housing coordinator Charles Palmer to see what might be done to defuse the situation. Already, East Coast newspapers were not only covering the developing story but also editorializing on behalf of black occupancy.

Before it was determined who would join the delegation, as well as attend to the logistics associated with such a trip, a document titled "Statement on Sojourner Truth Housing Project" was crafted by the Reverend Hill and signed by thirty-seven prominent local supporters:

We strongly protest the barring of Negro defense workers from the Sojourner Truth housing project as an act disruptive of the unity of our people, which jeopardizes the defense of our Nation.

The Sojourner Truth project was expressly planned for and promised to the Negro defense workers of our city, in recognition of the especially critical housing problem faced by this group. A Negro manager has been chosen for the project; not only that, but a substantial number of Negro families had already been selected for occupancy in it.

In his recent message to the Congress and the American people, President Roosevelt warned us that if we are to achieve victory in our war for freedom "We must guard against divisions among ourselves. We must be particularly vigilant against racial discrimination in any of its ugly forms."

The denial of the Sojourner Truth project to the Negro defense workers for whom it was originally intended is precisely the sort of dangerously divisive action so strongly condemned by the President. We demand that this discriminatory decision be reversed.[51]

The statement was widely disseminated locally and sent to various federal officials as well. The STCC was now seriously on the offensive, with precious time ticking off the clock. Everyone knew the housing units were almost ready for occupation, and once the first residents were assigned their units and began the move-in process, it would be nearly impossible to reverse course. All local levers of power seemed to be exhausted. The DHC was reluctant to officially voice any recommendations beyond what it had already done since its relationship with federal authorities was complicated by mixed messages and contradictory policies. No use causing further deterioration in the relationship with the USHA, FWA and DDH. However, the mayor had become outspoken of late and seemed prepared to take on a larger role on the issue. Members of the STCC approached Mayor Jeffries directly on January 29, and after a short meeting, he agreed to send off a letter to Washington. First, however, he needed a resolution coming from the DHC in support of black occupancy; otherwise, he was afraid that federal authorities might conclude there was a serious division in city government. Though a couple commissioners declined to sign off, he obtained the signatures of most of the housing commissioners. He was now prepared to draft the following letter to Baird Snyder, Charles F. Palmer and Colonel F. Charles Starr, using his recent remarks before the Detroit City Common Council as a template:

> *Our Detroit Housing Commission was instructed last week to accept applications for the Sojourner Truth defense housing project from white persons.*
>
> *To refresh your memory, for months the tenant selection division of the Detroit Housing Commission has been accepting and investigating applications from Negroes. In fact, from the inception of this project the housing commission, together with the informed citizenry of Detroit, was of the opinion that this was to be a Negro defense housing project. Since our instructions to change this to a white project, a cursory but yet a relatively complete survey of the city has been made for the purpose of locating an alternative Negro project. No place apparently is available with anything like the same satisfaction. In fact it appears that to build a project with any size with the requirements laid down by the Defense Housing Authority as to vacant land, it seems necessary to go beyond the borders of the city.*
>
> *Therefore I have discussed this matter at length with the members of the Common Council of the City of Detroit, and we feel that the Defense Housing Authority has made a mistake in diverting this to a white project, and that in fairness to the Negro population of the city of Detroit and the Negro defense workers, this project should be maintained as a Negro defense housing program.*
>
> *We earnestly request you to authorize the housing commission of Detroit to place Negro defense workers in the Sojourner Truth project.*[52]

At an emergency meeting of the STCC on the same day, over $1,200 was raised to send a biracial delegation of thirty-seven citizens to Washington that very night. Made up of civic, labor and church leaders, the delegation set its sights on Baird Snyder, who had replaced Clark Foreman. While no official statement was issued in the aftermath of the meeting the next day, members of the delegation believed they had made their point. On Monday, February 2, just eighteen days after the earlier reversal, Charles F. Palmer, defense housing coordinator, announced that the Sojourner Truth Homes would be re-designated for black occupancy.

Likely never to be resolved is the issue of what specifically tipped the balance and caused federal authorities to reverse their decision yet again on occupancy of Sojourner Truth. Was it the mayor's letter? The STCC delegation meeting with Baird Snyder? The influence of Eleanor Roosevelt? Media attention, both local and national? Behind-the-scenes lobbying by members of the Black Cabinet? The labor unions? NAACP? NUL? What is certain is that federal authorities, now reversing their decision, would remain unmoved, despite the anticipated backlash soon to follow from white residents in the area of Nevada and Fenelon.

THE RIOT AND ITS AFTERMATH

Upon learning of the federal housing project re-designation, Joseph Buffa and the SMFHIA organized a rapid response. Approximately seventy-five protesters, mostly women, stormed city hall, forcing their way into Mayor Jeffries's office. The mayor promised them that the city council would hear them Wednesday. Ignoring this commitment, the crowd marched into council chambers demanding an immediate hearing. Continuous shouting from the crowd made discussion or explanation difficult for council members, though Councilman George Edwards made one point clear to everyone in attendance—that the leaders of this assembly, Buffa and Dalzell, were "inflamers of racial hatred in Detroit....They are persons whose sole interest is in the few lots on which they will lose a little money. They are doing this community a distinct disservice when unity is important."[53] The major complaint of the crowd, however, was that the mayor had indicated earlier that he lacked any authority to act on the matter, and then, most recently, he had persuaded the council to support his petition directed at the defense housing authorities to switch the project back from white to black occupancy. In an impassioned rebuttal, Jeffries asserted,

> After the Federal officials selected this site against our advice, there was no right way to do the job. It was mishandled from the beginning. Whatever the cause, it became our problem. It was up to us to do something about it. Let's talk practically about the matter. Most Negroes didn't come to this

country because they wanted to—they were brought here. We fought a Civil War over this problem, and we passed the thirteenth amendment to the Constitution which guarantees them equal opportunity.[54]

Some small satisfaction was achieved by the protesters during the hearing when Councilman Charles Dorais, well known in Detroit's Catholic circles, indicated he might be willing to change his mind in favor of white occupancy of the project, provided that a suitable alternative site could be found for the black defense workers.

The impromptu hearing did not break off until late Tuesday afternoon, but not without threats of returning the next morning to bring the controversy to a more favorable resolution. Many protesters remained at city hall and picketed outside the building for another hour or two before breaking up and heading home for the evening.

On the same day as the city council protest, DHC director-secretary Charles Edgecomb announced that the first sixty-five families were to move into the project on Friday, February 14, but that because of delays created by the recent controversy, the move-in might have to be postponed.

Sojourner Truth Homes at the corner of Nevada and Fenelon on Detroit's northeast side. *Library of Congress.*

The very next day, Councilman Dorais proposed a compromise settlement that was immediately supported by fellow councilmen William G. Rogell, Eugene I. Van Antwerp and James H. Garlick. Dorais believed he could persuade the Ford Motor Company to revise its plans to build a defense plant at Dequindre and Modern and move defense work to a neighboring site, but there was a catch: a decision regarding a potential new housing project on this site had to be made by Monday, February 16, as the auto company was working under time constraints of its own.

On Tuesday, February 10, Mayor Jeffries apprised federal housing officials of this site availability for a limited period. Even though he was acting on a request by these four city council members, he made very clear to each of them he was not recommending abandonment of black occupancy at Fenelon and Nevada. His telegram to defense officials was carefully phrased so as not to recommend one choice or the other:

> *Members of our City Council have requested me to inform you that the original Negro housing site at Dequindre and Modern streets is now available under an option expiring next Monday.*
>
> *Please wire us at once your decision as to acceptance of this site and also your desires as to type of occupancy for Sojourner Truth in view of this development. We as your agents will proceed in accordance with instructions. Monday option expiration date makes immediate and definite answer from you imperative.*[55]

Several telegrams from black leaders in Detroit to Mayor Jeffries made quite clear that regardless of what transpired at Dequindre and Modern, they were not abandoning the present Sojourner Truth project at Fenelon and Nevada earmarked for black settlement and hoped the mayor had not abandoned the plan either. At this point, it was not just about finding housing for black defense workers; it was about no longer being treated as second-class citizens.

The publication and distribution of the *Seven Mile–Fenelon Homeowners News*—a one-time issue—on February 14 drew widespread attention in both white and black communities, threatening to further aggravate an already tense situation. The *News* directly warned of an impending race riot stemming from any attempted black occupancy of Sojourner Truth. It further ridiculed the mayor, the common council and the housing commission for being pawns in the hands of such external agents as the NAACP and the Communist Party. Highlighting the tabloid was an announcement of

HELP THE WHITE PEOPLE

To Keep This District WHITE

MEN

NEEDED

TO KEEP OUR LINES SOLID

COME TO NEVADA and FENLON

Sunday and Monday

WE NEED HELP

Don't BE YELLOW   COME OUT

We Need Every WHITE MAN

WE WANT OUR GIRLS TO WALK ON THE STREET NOT RAPED

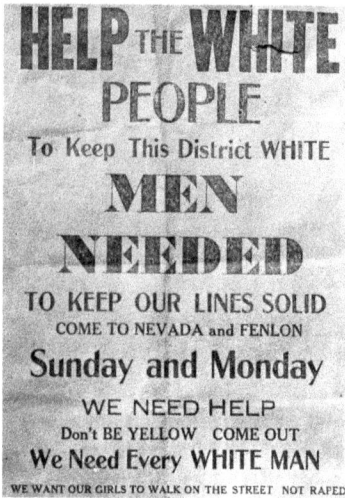

Flier distributed by the Seven Mile–Fenelon Association pressure group organized against black occupancy of Sojourner Truth Homes. *Walter P. Reuther Library, Archives of Labor and Urban Affairs, Wayne State University.*

a mass meeting at Cass Technical High School on Wednesday, February 18, at 8:00 p.m. Local authorities feared the rally would simply be a pretext for planning a physical confrontation should any black defense workers attempt occupation of Sojourner Truth. Joseph Buffa was brought in for questioning by Wayne County chief assistant prosecutor Julian G. McIntosh following complaints that, by virtue of statements made in the publication, he was inciting a riot. Buffa was released with an admonition to refrain from making any inflammatory statements at the mass meeting. He indicated he would be reading from a prepared statement.

The day following the rally at Cass Tech, a mêlée occurred at city hall as a contingent of approximately one hundred white protesters, principally women, cornered Mayor Jeffries in the corridor outside city council chambers. Jeffries had just read to council members a telegram authored by Baird Snyder in response to a resolution adopted by council urging a further delay of black occupancy at Sojourner Truth. The telegram brushed aside the request for delay and reaffirmed federal instructions to begin moving families into the project. Escorted by police officers, Jeffries made his way back to his office on the first floor, but two officers remained stationed outside to bar members of the throng from pushing their way inside.

Meanwhile, DHC's Director Edgecomb declared that while a few preliminary steps needed to be completed, the first African American families should be moving into the project on Monday, February 23. Edgecomb met later that afternoon with DHC members to confirm execution of the federal order. By unanimous vote, the housing commission agreed to abide by the order of Baird Snyder and approved the final list of black occupants for the project. However, at the conclusion of the commission hearing, Edgecomb to make moving arrangements and obtain coal to heat their apartments.

John Dalzell, unable to persuade the mayor to support a short delay in occupancy, announced that if efforts failed to stop black tenants from moving

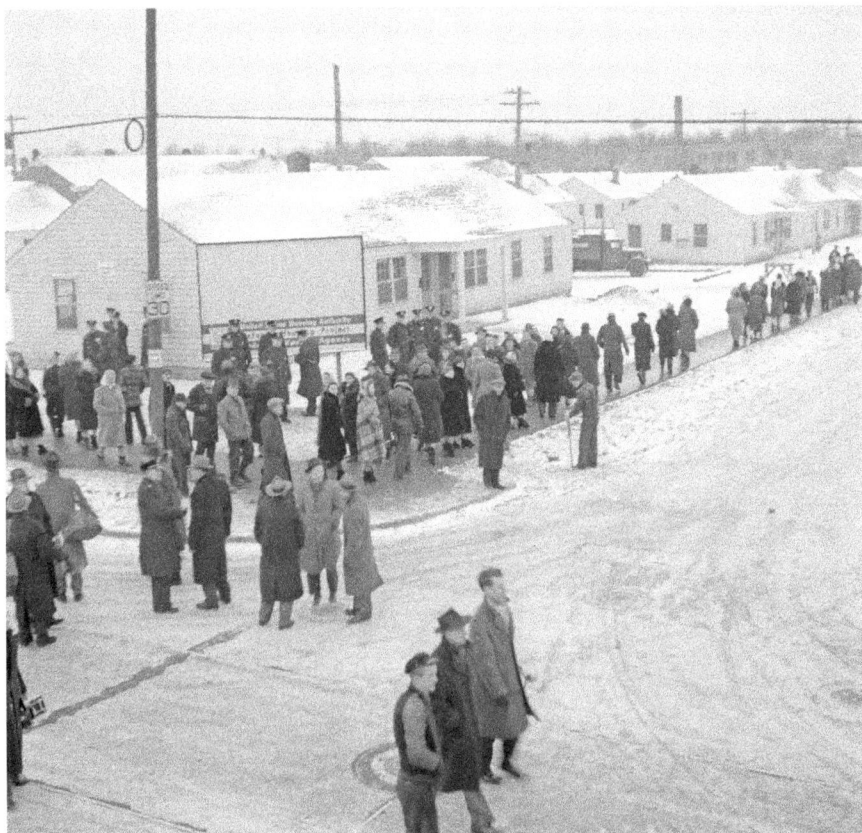

White picketers at the corner of Nevada and Fenelon protesting the assignment of black
war workers to this new federal war housing facility, February 1942. *Library of Congress.*

into Sojourner Truth, he would seek the recall of Mayor Jeffries. As Dalzell
plotted his next steps, Rudolph Tenerowicz was delivering a speech on the
floor of the House of Representatives berating Mayor Jeffries and claiming
that communists were behind a campaign to make the new Sojourner Truth
housing project an African American development. He specifically singled
out sixteen signatories affixed to the petition that the Citizens Committee
had sent off to federal authorities as "listed conspicuously" in the records
of the House Un-American Activities Committee, chaired by conservative
Texas Democrat Martin Dies. "This false leadership," Tenerowicz asserted,
"may as well be brought out into the open and exposed for what it really is—
rabble-rousing, publicity seeking, ambitious radicals bent on the destruction
of human values and property values alike."[56]

THREAT BECOMES REALITY

The very next day, February 20, after all the denials of incitement and all the posturing, Detroit's worst fears were realized. The dreaded riot had begun at the site of the recently completed Sojourner Truth Homes.

At 6:00 a.m. on the day when twenty-four families were to be moved into the project, a group of picketers was parading around the southeastern entrance, and within two hours, the ranks had swelled to five hundred. White picketers were determined to prevent the move-in from occurring. A single truck loaded with the first tenant's furniture moved on past the project after a picket talked with the driver. At intersections distant from the project, several other furniture trucks were turned away by groups of picketers. The trucks parked, however, near the intersection of Ryan and Nevada, awaiting further instructions from police.

At a home near the intersection where the moving trucks had parked, a group of African American men was observed in the backyard using hammers

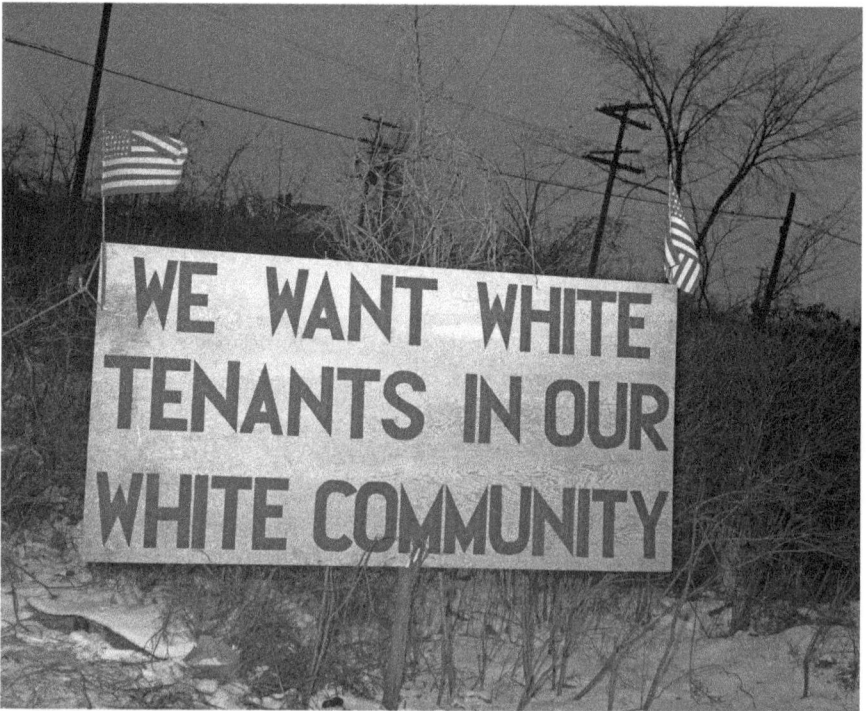

Large sign installed surreptitiously across the street from the Sojourner Truth housing project at Nevada and Fenelon Streets in northeast Detroit. *Library of Congress.*

Police attempt to disperse rioting crowds with tear gas on the streets near the Sojourner Truth Homes. *Walter P. Reuther Library, Archives of Labor and Urban Affairs, Wayne State University.*

to break up concrete block into pieces. A few others were transporting the pieces to the corner, where they were piled up and ready for use as need be. A detail of 150 foot and mounted patrolmen was assigned to supervise the move-in, but when rock throwing began, Superintendent Louis Berg ordered all available men from nearby precincts to the scene.

Clearly outmanned, police consulted with black and white leaders to keep the violence from getting out of hand. In the meantime, volleys of shotgun fire could be heard near the intersection as police fired tear gas bombs to disperse the growing crowd at the Ryan-Nevada intersection, where most of the activity was occurring. Early on, seven whites and seven blacks were injured in the mêlée and required immediate attention at local hospitals. But the toll would later rise. Among the African Americans, Henry Love, Edward Siebert, Fred Ware and Malvin Clark were being treated for head injuries at Receiving Hospital. Clarence Caviness suffered a fractured shoulder. Two other injured African Americans, William Pearson and Lawrence Martin, were held at the hospital as police prisoners after both were alleged to be carrying .32-caliber revolvers on their persons.[57]

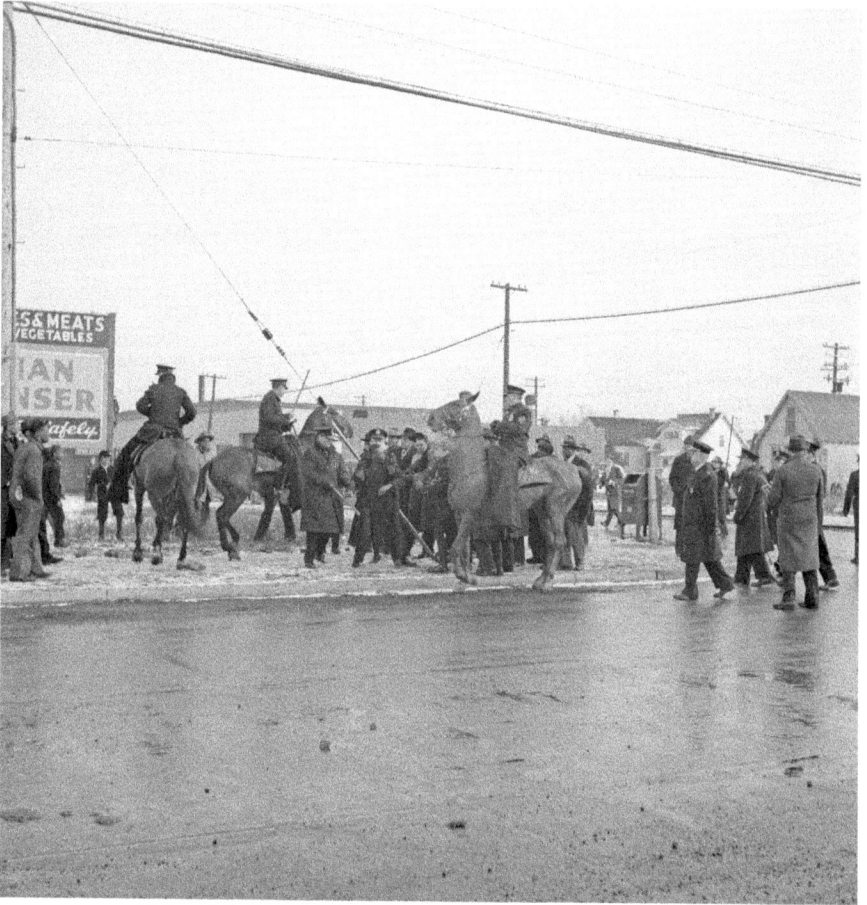

Above: Detroit police on horseback attempting to disperse a group of protesters at the intersection of Nevada and Ryan Roads. *Library of Congress.*

Opposite, top: African American men confront Detroit police detective about uneven treatment at the hands of police during the riot on February 28 at the Sojourner Truth housing project. *Library of Congress.*

Opposite, bottom: Five African American men stand on sidewalk with their hands raised above their heads, with uniformed officers facing them in foreground. *Walter P. Reuther Library, Archives of Labor and Urban Affairs, Wayne State University.*

Among the whites injured in early rioting and taken to Saratoga Hospital was Walter Efimetz, who suffered a stab wound in the back. A woman, Dolores Hommer, was taken to St. Francis Hospital in Hamtramck with head wounds. The remaining white persons injured were patrolmen. Patrolman Carl Mayer suffered a six-inch gash behind his left ear after being knocked from his horse by a brick. Joining him at Saratoga was patrolman Joseph Dunn, also suffering head injuries. Patrolman Edward Koss was treated for head injuries at St. Francis Hospital. The two other patrolmen, Terry Mason and Thomas Turklay, were quickly dispatched to Harper Hospital with facial injuries.[58]

Despite an announcement to the crowd that Mayor Jeffries had decided to indefinitely postpone the scheduled occupation, the two groups—still in large numbers—remained at the intersection. Commissioner White made a plea directly to the black crowd to disperse, but there was very little movement. Director Edgecomb tried to break up the group of white protesters by assuring them that that there would be "no sneak moves"— that is, they would be notified in advance of any future attempt to move in the African American families. As with the black crowd, the whites kept

Police officers on horseback attempting crowd control during early morning hours of February 28, 1942, at corner of Nevada and Ryan Roads. *Library of Congress.*

Above: Black man arrested and escorted to police car to be taken to local precinct for processing. *Library of Congress.*

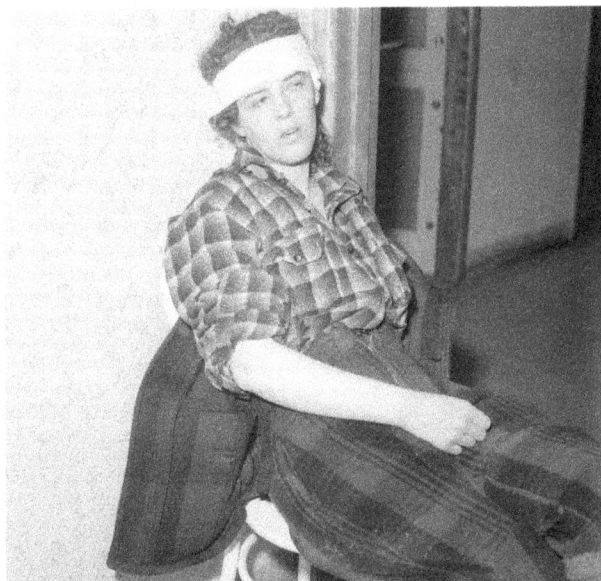

Left: White woman identified as Dolores Hommer sits back in chair with a bandage wrapped around her head in the aftermath of the violent protest over the Sojourner Truth projects. *Walter P. Reuther Library, Archives of Labor and Urban Affairs, Wayne State University.*

Crowd of young white men surround an overturned automobile that attempted to break a picket line during the Sojourner Truth Housing Riot. *Walter P. Reuther Library, Archives of Labor and Urban Affairs, Wayne State University.*

their ground, with both groups shouting epithets and taunting each other across the newly established police lines.

The standoff was broken by several incidents that produced serious injuries. At 2:30 p.m., approximately three dozen black youths, one armed with a pickaxe, tried to push through the police lines and confront the whites on the other side. Police were able to subdue the youth with the pickaxe and chase the remaining youths into nearby fields. At almost the same time, two cars with blacks drove into the white section but withdrew when several cars with whites intercepted them.

At about 3:30 p.m., three African Americans were walking east on Nevada toward the project. At Justine Avenue, a group of whites impeded their progress and a fight ensued. Two detectives driving past were able to end the brawl, but not before one of the black men was struck with a length of iron pipe and transported to St. Francis Hospital for treatment. A white man, Bernard Augustyniak, was immediately arrested and subsequently booked on a charge of felonious assault.

Just half an hour later, a car with three black occupants approached the intersection of Stockton and Shields Avenues. They continued in the direction of a group of several dozen white pickets. Police were on the scene turning cars around and away from the intersection. However, the car accelerated, jumped the curb and nearly struck the pickets. Police

Police take real estate developer Joseph Buffa into custody for his role in instigating the Sojourner Truth Housing Riot on February 28, 1942. *Library of Congress.*

immediately apprehended the driver and his two companions and placed them under arrest. As they were being transported to the Davison Station, a small group of pickets overturned the vehicle and proceeded to smash the windows and do severe damage to the body.

Perhaps the most serious incident of the afternoon occurred when a truck loaded with club-wielding African Americans broke through police lines and headed east on Nevada. When confronted by a crowd of white protestors, the truck turned onto a side street, whereupon the blacks jumped from the truck and several fights ensued. Only with great difficulty were police able to subdue the combatants. With blood streaming down their faces, several black and white participants required medical attention.

Random confrontations between individuals and groups of combatants continued throughout the evening. Police were clearly unwilling to disperse the large crowd of white protestors who refused to leave. Despite assurances otherwise, the picketers were of one mind: the moment they dispersed or looked the other way, some tenant assigned a specific housing unit would sneak in to begin habitation, changing the whole calculus status quo. They were not budging, at least not on move-in day.

As the situation in northeast Detroit remained volatile, Reverend Hill called for a meeting of the Citizens Committee at Plymouth Congregational Church to assess what had unfolded on this day and plot a strategy moving forward. Among the more than three hundred members who attended the 8:00 p.m. meeting, there was consensus that local authorities—from

Harold Dillard, fourteen, is arrested by police officers during the Sojourner Truth Housing Riot as his sister clings to him in his defense. *Walter P. Reuther Library, Archives of Labor and Urban Affairs, Wayne State University.*

the mayor's office on down to the patrolman on the street—were either unwilling or unable to enforce the federal mandate. However, there would be no capitulation. The mayor was simply going to have to turn the matter over to the federal authorities and call in federal troops as necessary. Lest there be any confusion or miscommunication between Reverend Hill and Mayor Jeffries, by the end of the meeting, members of the Citizens

An African American man runs in front of a police vehicle, with a uniformed police officer holding his nightstick up behind him and houses in the background in the aftermath of the violent protest over the Sojourner Truth projects. *Walter P. Reuther Library, Archives of Labor and Urban Affairs, Wayne State University.*

Committee charged Reverend Hill with the immediate task of wiring the White House and requesting federal troops to ensure the orderly movement of rent-paying tenants into the assigned apartments at Sojourner Truth Homes without delay.

THE IMMEDIATE AFTERMATH

Sunday morning brought peace and quiet to northeast Detroit as pickets had begun to break up during the early morning hours, despite earlier avowals otherwise. Nonetheless, Police Superintendent Louis Berg kept 120 patrolmen posted in the vicinity of the project. Many of the Roman Catholic pickets made it to midmorning Mass at St. Louis the King Parish in time to hear Father Dzink's homily on the righteousness of the cause at hand. Most of those suffering injuries had now been released from various hospital emergency rooms in the area, and more than one hundred blacks were sitting in holding cells pending court examinations Monday morning. The twenty-four black families scheduled for the previous day's move-in could not, in most cases, return to their previous living arrangements. Housing was so tight in the city that as soon as one tenant departed a unit, another tenant moved in, typically the very same day. The DHC was hard-pressed to locate temporary accommodations for these project-approved tenants but did manage to find space in either the Brewster Homes or in the buildings of the unfinished Brewster-Douglass Apartments for most of them. The DHC sincerely hoped that *temporary* was a reliable descriptor.

The Detroit Police Special Investigation Squad, under the command of Inspector George McLellan, reported that 108 individuals had been arrested during the mêlée; 6 faced charges of felonious assault, 24 of carrying concealed weapons such as handguns and blackjacks and 79 of inciting a riot. Perhaps hoping to tamp down claims of discrimination, McLellan reported to the press that only about half of those arrested in the demonstrations were black, when in fact nearly all were black. Only 3 whites were charged with various offenses. Although the tally had not been formalized, it was believed that 40 individuals were injured in the rioting, including 3 mounted policemen. In addition, three police horses were injured, two having been struck with clubs and a third stabbed.

At arraignment on Monday morning, the first wave of defendants faced either recorder's court judges George Murphy or W. McKay Skillman: 52 of the 108 arrested in Saturday's riot were brought to court, 25 on charges of carrying concealed weapons and the rest for disturbing the peace. The first 4, all black, came before Judge Murphy and were accused of disturbing the peace. Their attorneys argued that whites were illegally picketing the project in the first place and that consequently no peace existed for the blacks to disturb. Judge Murphy ruled there was insufficient evidence to prove that they had disturbed the peace by inciting to riot. Judge Murphy dismissed the charges in twenty-four cases and adjourned three others until Wednesday for further testimony. Meanwhile, the concealed weapons cases came before Judge Skillman. The 24 defendants pleaded innocent and demanded examinations. They were all held under $1,000 bonds pending examinations set for March 9, 10 and 11.[59]

A NATIONAL AND INTERNATIONAL ISSUE

Without needing to consult with representatives of any organization or group, Mayor Jeffries had reached the conclusion independently that Sojourner Truth Homes, being federal property, would now require direct federal intervention in some form. The specific form he did not envision, but he hoped that through direct consultation with John Blandford, the head of the newly organized National Housing Administration, a solution would be found. He decided to meet with Blandford on Tuesday and fly out to Washington as soon as possible.

Since Jeffries was to be in Washington, he thought it prudent to meet with Martin McIntyre, secretary to President Roosevelt, to keep the White House firmly in the loop. He also agreed to meet Congressman Tenerowicz later in the day, but only after receiving satisfaction from key officials of the National Housing Administration. It was Jeffries's intent to place the matter squarely in the hands of federal authorities, and the two men he arranged to meet—John Blandford, the top man at the agency, and Leon Kyserling, the director of the public housing division—were precisely the officials who could resolve the issue once and for all.

Accompanying the mayor to the meeting were City Controller Charles Oakman and Max Barton of the WPA's Detroit office. As they were leaving the Washington Hotel to make their way to the offices of the NHA, they were accosted by Joseph Buffa, John Dalzell, Virgil Chandler and the Reverend John Hopkins, the latter of North Detroit Baptist Church. Buffa and his entourage insisted that they be at the table during this important, decisive meeting with the NHA. Jeffries refused this demand.

Beyond resolving a local housing issue, the importance of the meeting was not lost on Blandford and Kyserling. The national policy implications were already apparent and were beginning to reverberate throughout the halls of the NHA. Jeffries made it clear to federal officials—and Congressman Tenerowicz, who would sit in on the late afternoon meeting—that he doubted the ability of Detroit police to prevent a recurrence of conditions that had just occurred the previous Saturday. "I feel like MacArthur in the Philippines," Jeffries was quoted as saying. "I'm responsible in the field but the decision is made in Washington." For their part, Blandford and Kyserling would concede that Secretary of the Interior Ickes's policy—adopted by the USHA—of not permitting projects that might "change the character of a neighborhood" had been disregarded when the Sojourner Truth Homes had been designated an

African American project. Interference outside the control of housing administration, it was suggested, came from some other federal entity. Neither Blandford nor Kyserling would point fingers, but they clearly implied that none of the present controversy would have occurred if the original decision to locate the defense housing project designated for black occupancy had been at some other location than the racially mixed Nevada and Fenelon neighborhood. In previous federal practice, mixed areas were typically designated white, thus further promoting the official federal policy of segregation while exacerbating an already critical housing shortage for African American defense workers.

Undoubtedly, incidents such as the Sojourner Truth housing controversy threatened to weaken homefront morale and make American groups fear or hate one another. Such behavior, it was feared, might lead to workplace disruption, strikes or anything that could cut back military production. Such racial discord did not go unnoticed in the offices of German, Italian and Japanese propagandists, who, like their American counterparts in the Office of War Information, waged a different kind of war against the enemy: to sow the seeds of division and doubt among its citizenry. Early in the war, for example, Radio Tokyo broadcast throughout Asia an unsettling reality of the American South:

> *It is a singular fact that supposedly civilized Americans in these times deny the Negroes the opportunity to engage in respectable jobs, the right of access to restaurants, theaters or the same train accommodations as themselves, and will periodically run amuck to lynch Negroes individually or to slaughter them wholesale—old men, women, and children alike—in race wars like the present one.*[60]

During the winter of 1942, shortwave recordings in Washington revealed that the Nazis were using the Sojourner Truth housing dispute for propaganda in South American countries. Tokyo Radio, on the other hand, was in Dutch, directed to the Dutch East Indies:

> *Because of the labor shortage in the United States, many people have moved to Detroit. This has made it necessary for the Government to order white homeowners to admit Negro war workers. But when the Negroes attempted to move in, they were shot at by whites and bloody street riots resulted and there were many dead and wounded.*[61]

126

The NHA was now deeply concerned that the Sojourner Truth controversy could set off race riots in several cities. Similar controversies existed in at least half a dozen Northern industrial centers and others in the border states of Delaware, Kentucky, Maryland, Missouri and West Virginia. Officials were fielding scores of telephone calls and answering numerous letters and telegrams, all of which were inquiring about federal strategy going forward. Aggravating the situation, however, were accusations of conspiracy that were gaining traction in various communities, and the ones being made in Detroit were particularly difficult to suppress because of just enough anecdotal evidence to make them plausible. John Williams, for example, a Detroit-based correspondent for the influential *Pittsburgh Courier*, suggested that real estate interests in the area, not white citizens, were behind the picketing and that DHC director Charles Edgecomb had capitulated to these interests. The Reverend White charged that a deeper conspiracy was afoot, a conspiracy of forces opposed to democracy. White contended that the police were likely in on it, given the fact that they made no effort to disperse the crowd of whites and that no attempt was made to stop a fiery cross from being burned at the site. Harper Poulson, of the Citizens Committee, asserted that the riot had been carefully orchestrated. The police were aware, he argued, of plans hatched at Ku Klux Klan meetings and at a meeting of the Seven Mile–Fenelon Neighborhood Association. The NHA realized the only counter it had to these theories was to decide regarding black occupancy as soon as possible.

Before any official announcement was made regarding resolution of the issue at Sojourner Truth, the NHA received several proposals that found their way into the local press. One such proposal called for the federal government to purchase the land lying between Sojourner Truth and Conant Gardens. The land would be held for future development as an African American settlement. Any local antagonism could be resolved by offering white homeowners in the immediate area the opportunity to dispose of their properties at fair market prices. Purportedly, some NHA officials supported this solution. Another proposal, put forward by Congressman Tenerowicz, relegated the project buildings to city offices. If that didn't appeal to Mayor Jeffries, perhaps the army and navy should be consulted on the possibility of using the project for military housing. The latter proposal had been suggested by City Councilman Dorais, who had been in communication with Captain R. Thornton Brodhead, commanding officer of the naval reserve in Michigan and in charge of the Detroit Naval Armory. Broadhead acknowledged a deep interest in using the project to accommodate the families of enlisted navy personnel in Detroit, as they were having serious difficulties finding suitable quarters in Detroit. Ultimately, all of the proposals were rejected for one reason or another. Blandford had already made his decision, and there would be no turning back.[62]

Blandford, however, felt that a cooling-off period was necessary, as no formal announcement regarding the timing of occupancy at Sojourner Truth would be forthcoming for nearly six weeks. This is not to suggest that the issue was being ignored in Washington. Blandford had a few conversations with Mayor Jeffries and leaders of national organizations like the NAACP and NUL that he felt could help control the narrative going forward. He was not interested in engaging the Seven Mile–Fenelon crowd; he knew he could never satisfy their demands.

In Detroit, the Citizens Committee remained active, interacting frequently with representatives of the NAACP and NUL and receiving assurances that nothing of consequence had changed in Washington. Both small organizational meetings and large mass gatherings, with as many as three thousand attendees, were held to exchange views and, more importantly, to solicit funds to provide for legal representation for the remaining African Americans who were facing charges. Meanwhile, the DHC remained in the loop as well, as Reverend White communicated with the Citizens Committee regarding any discussions about the project taking place during commission meetings.

More cases of alleged individual wrongdoing during the February 28 riot came before the bench during the interim. Most cases were quickly dismissed, leaving but nineteen cases involving African American suspects. By the end of March, charges against nine defendants were dropped, and seven other defendants were placed on probation for eighteen months. Another pleaded guilty to carrying a concealed weapon and was sentenced to two and a half to five years. Of the final two African American defendants, one received eight months' probation for weapons possession, and the other, a repeat offender, was sentenced to a prison term of one year and a day.

Of three white rioters who were arrested, only one, Bernard Augustyniak, faced charges for felonious assault, for striking a man with an iron rod. Augustyniak received two years' probation. Charges against the other two white defendants were dropped.

GRAND JURY INVESTIGATION

Meanwhile, a federal grand jury investigation into the cause of the February 28 riot was begun almost immediately. Impaneled for just over a month, the grand jury handed down three indictments on charges of seditious conspiracy. Warrants were issued on Friday, April 17, for Parker Sage, treasurer of the National Workers League (NWL); Garland L. Alderman, secretary of the NWL; and Virgil Chandler, executive vice president of the Seven Mile–Fenelon Homeowners Improvement Association. (The National Workers League was founded in Detroit in 1938 by Parker Sage and sought worker membership to support its anti-Semitic and racist program of "equal rights" for whites and certain other "non-Jews." It sought to adopt "clean racial standards which shall permanently guarantee that Americans of white European descent shall in the future direct the political and economic destiny of America." The organization, with a relatively small membership, openly espoused fascist doctrine and praised Nazism and, as such, had drawn the attention of the House Committee on Un-American Activities.)[63]

Named as co-conspirators but not indicted were Joseph Buffa, president of the SMFHIA; John Dalzell, secretary; Fred Monasterski, a vice president; and Leonard Stewart, also a vice president.

The indictment set up two counts, one charging that the defendants violated the civil rights of black tenants of the Sojourner Truth Homes by preventing them from occupying the premises on which they held leases and the other charging seditious conspiracy in preventing, hindering and delaying execution of a U.S. law. The civil rights count provided for a maximum penalty of a $5,000 fine and ten years in prison, and the other count called for a maximum penalty of a $5,000 fine and six years' imprisonment.

It was alleged that the defendants conspired to "injure, oppress, threaten and intimidate certain individuals and other citizens of the United States in the free exercise and enjoyment of the rights and privileges secured them by the Constitution"; that part of the conspiracy was for the defendants to appear before the Common Council and the Detroit Housing Commission to protest occupancy of Sojourner Truth by black war workers and to threaten that there would be bloodshed and rioting if the blacks tried to occupy the buildings.

The indictment further alleged that Sage, Alderman and Chandler incited numerous other persons to maintain a picket line at the project and to use force and threats of force. The defendants appeared at numerous meetings of the SMFHIA and other organizations to incite persons to volunteer for picket duty and arranged for a signal, namely the sounding of automobile horns, to summon the pickets. They conspired to establish such a tight picket line at the project that any effort to get through it would and did result in bloodshed and rioting. Since the time of the riot, the defendants continued to appear at meetings of the SMFHIA to maintain a picket line.

The indictment was returned before federal judge Frank A. Picard. No connection was established between the National Workers League and the SMFHIA as organizations, nor was the league involved in the conspiracy.

THE FEDERAL ANNOUNCEMENT AND MOVE-IN

Finally, on April 15, fully six weeks after the housing project riot, the federal government made its official final announcement regarding the disposition of the Sojourner Truth Homes. John Blandford instructed the Detroit Housing Commission to proceed with filling the housing project with African American occupants. Moreover, he placed the responsibility for effecting the move on city government. At the conclusion of the telegram, Blandford directed the DHC to notify city government of the contemplated action so that the city could initiate measures to ensure a smooth occupancy.

Blandford then called Jeffries to instruct him not to take any action regarding the move-in until and unless he conferred with Governor Van Wagoner. Jeffries was stunned to learn that the burden of protection of the African American occupants fell, once again, on the city's resources, and the question of contacting the governor to seek additional resources went without saying. The Detroit Police Department was in no position to supervise the move-in by itself, especially after considering the potential of a second round of organized resistance. Jeffries immediately contacted the governor's office and arranged a conference at noon the following day at the East Lansing post of the state police. Accompanying Jeffries were Charles Edgecomb of the DHC and police commissioner Frank Eaman. Though he had tendered his resignation right after hearing of the contents of Blandford's telegram to the DHC, Eaman agreed to participate in the conference as one of his final official acts of office.

At the East Lansing meeting, the four conferees quickly concluded that federal or state troops would be necessary to keep the peace. The first group of African American families holding leases would be safely moved into the Sojourner Truth Homes under the protection of state troops and battalions of city and state police. The governor subsequently, at state expense, authorized the deployment of 1,500 Michigan Home Guard drawn from twenty-four companies, ten from Detroit and the other fourteen from outstate. These troops would be supplemented by 300 state police and 450 Detroit patrolmen. For two days before the planned move on April 29, state troops were arriving at the staging area set up at the state fairgrounds at Eight Mile and Woodward Avenue. There the troops would drill and receive instruction on military procedure with respect to engaging civilians.

And so, just after midnight on April 29, Home Guard troops took their positions, circling tightly around the housing project. At the break of dawn, state police arrived in more than fifty vehicles to survey the area, looking out for any potential disturbance. A convoy of moving vans slowly turned down Nevada Avenue, surrounded on both sides by police motorcycles. Detroit police patrolmen took positions at each major intersection around the project and prevented onlookers from gathering in groups.

The first family to move into Sojourner Truth Homes was Walter Jackson and his wife, Queenetta. Clinging closely to their mother were the two youngest of five children. Cautious and concerned for the safety of his family but resolute about claiming his civil right to move in, Jackson told a reporter, "I have only got one time to die, and I'd just as soon die here." Jackson would not have to die on this day, as the move-in went smoothly.

Joseph Battle, with his wife and four children, moved into the project next, without incident. The remaining twelve families of defense workers scheduled for this day's mass move-in arrived and completed the process by midafternoon.[64]

While there was no violence, there were individuals ready to stir things up if the opportunity arose. Small groups, mostly women, milled about on the south side along Nevada Avenue. Aside from hurling insults at police or the moving vans or the African American defense workers, nothing came of it. However, the crowd was bigger at the north side of the project where the realtor and SMFHIA president was provoking an already agitated crowd. Police moved in and immediately took Buffa and a dozen others into custody. They would be released later in the afternoon at the

Moving vans escorted by Detroit police motorcycle units on April 29, 1942, as African American war workers prepare to finally move into the Sojourner Truth Homes. *Library of Congress.*

Moving van breaks down on Nevada Road as Michigan Home Guard march in a westerly direction. *Library of Michigan.*

Soldiers standing fifty feet apart to ensure that the Sojourner Truth Homes is completely surrounded and protected against any protesters choosing to disrupt the start of the move-in by tenants. *Library of Congress.*

Davison station with one exception, Taylor Smith, who was being held on a concealed weapons charge.

That evening, three hundred white residents in the neighborhood of the project met at the parish hall of St. Louis the King Church to commiserate about the day's events. The rally was organized by Buffa and Virgil Chandler of the SMFHIA, both of whom denounced the unannounced move-in in direct violation of what they claimed was a promise of no "sneak move" by DHC's Charles Edgecomb. Since the first defense workers had already moved in under the watchful eye of

Members of Michigan Home Guard stopping and inspecting all vehicles before being allowed to proceed to Sojourner Truth Homes on move-in day, April 29, 1942. *Library of Congress.*

Sojourner Truth Homes methodically being settled, cars parked near units in background. *Library of Congress.*

Mother supervising placement of furniture as father watches over daughter in front of new housing unit. *Library of Congress.*

state troops, a grim sense of defeat settled over the crowd when someone asked about the next steps to be taken. No one really had an adequate answer.

In the days ahead, local police and state troops oversaw the new occupants as they directed the movers where to place furniture and other personal belongings in their new units. Children played outside on the frozen ground between the buildings. At day ten of the move-in, a gradual demobilization of state troops began and continued for another week until it was felt that the project was secure.

As a sort of exclamation point to events in the late winter and early spring of 1942 in northeast Detroit, Raymond Foley, state director of the

Proud family among the first to move into a new home at Sojourner Truth. *Library of Congress.*

Another family happy to pose for the camera on the stoop of their new home. *Library of Congress.*

Two-story brick unit in Sojourner Truth Homes. *Library of Congress.*

Federal Housing Administration, announced that FHA loans would be available to residents seeking mortgages in the neighborhoods surrounding Sojourner Truth Homes, thus removing one of the major objections to black occupancy by local white homeowners.

Conclusion

THE AFTERMATH

The Sojourner Truth housing controversy did not produce the long-term changes in federal policy for which progressive reformers had toiled. The expectation, in some liberal circles, was that because the riot was a wake-up call, surely federal officials were listening and ready to respond. Now, perhaps, the federal government would take an even stronger stand against discrimination and move—albeit slowly but deliberately—toward desegregation. In Washington, in a sense, officials *had* learned their lesson from the Detroit housing riot—just not the lesson progressives were advocating.

The neighborhood composition rule, formulated nearly a decade earlier by Secretary Harold Ickes and his associates, was still in play, but now it would need some tweaking. The original rule seemed clear enough: any public housing development, including defense housing, should not alter—but should reflect—the racial composition of the neighborhood in which it was to be built. In other words, projects to be built in formerly white neighborhoods would be exclusively white; in formerly black neighborhoods, exclusively black. If the Detroit experience had taught city planners anything at all, it was that neighborhoods that were previously mixed (typically working-class blacks and whites who needed to live near the factories to which they could walk) would become completely segregated by design, and the design would be formulated locally without federal interference. There would be no residual mix.

After Sojourner Truth, federal officials became keenly aware that the NHA, or any other agency of government, could not select a site and expect things to proceed smoothly without the approval of local residents. The federal government would provide funding and oversight for the housing project while the local housing commission, which was thought to best understand the local community, would be responsible for site and tenant selection as well as construction management. Federal officials left open to interpretation the infuriatingly vague word *neighborhood* that had been and could be interpreted as a reference to the immediate construction site, the entire square block or a much larger section of the city, such as the east side or the west side. It gave the local housing commissions much latitude in interpreting the desired degree of segregation.

Months after the Sojourner Truth controversy, the DHC had the opportunity to address official federal policy, past practice and future housing initiatives. A joint NAACP-NUL coalition wanted the DHC to conduct an open hearing on mixed occupancy, using data collected on two dozen instances where biracial neighborhoods had worked in cities around the country, but Mayor Jeffries interceded before the request could be made at a housing commission hearing. Furthermore, he requested the Common Council to reaffirm the neighborhood composition rule as official policy. After the council approved the mayor's recommendation, the DHC was quick to accept it. Jeffries strongly believed that the Sojourner Truth riot was the result of federal bungling; had they followed the recommendation of the DHC in the first place, the controversy never would have occurred. He failed to mention, however, that the Nevada-Fenelon site was the DHC's second choice.

Racial tensions did not subside after the last of the black defense workers and their families moved into the Sojourner Truth project. While there were no major racial incidents directly attributed to the move-in, the city continued to experience racial unrest on the streets, on the trolley cars and, most significantly, at employment centers.

At the time of his resignation, police commissioner Frank Eaman made clear that NHA director John Blandford had erred in ordering Detroit authorities to proceed with plans to move black defense workers into the project. Though he helped plan and execute the successful move-in, there is no evidence he changed his opinion about the designation of Sojourner Truth Homes as a black defense housing project. John H. Witherspoon was appointed commissioner on June 1 and would be best remembered

On a warm spring day, a grandmother is able to take her little granddaughter for a walk around the Sojourner Truth Homes without fear or concern following the rioting that occurred in late February. *Library of Congress.*

for presiding over the 1943 race riot in which 34 people were killed, 700 injured and 1,800 arrested. Property damage was estimated at $2 million (approximately $30 million in 2020 dollars). Witherspoon and other city administrators would blame "Negro hoodlums" for the violence, even though 17 of the 25 blacks—but none of the whites—were killed at the hands of Detroit Police. The NAACP would identify far deeper causes, including inadequate housing, employment discrimination and brutality from a predominantly white police force. Witherspoon would resign from the post five months after the riot.

CONCLUSION

In May, the design for a marble plaque to be affixed to the front of the Sojourner Truth administration building was presented for approval of the Detroit Housing Commission. Commissioner Harriet D. Kelly was still so indignant at federal officials for how the commission's original recommendations were ignored that she moved to strike not only the names of the commissioners but also any reference to the DHC. The other four commissioners were sympathetic to Kelly's sentiment but prevailed upon her to permit the inclusion of simply "The Detroit Housing Commission" without members' names.

Congressman Rudolph Tenerowicz would run unsuccessfully for reelection later in 1942. State senator Charles Diggs organized a disgruntled Citizens Committee and UAW leadership to promote former congressman George Sadowski during the Democratic primary. DHC member Reverend Horace White pushed for a black candidate, but Diggs, himself African American, persuaded the anti-Tenerowicz faction that only a white candidate could win. During the campaign, Tenerowicz was portrayed as an anti-black conservative to the First District voters. Sadowski would win both the Democratic primary and the November general election.

Black leaders in Detroit would push local prosecutors to move forward with the cases against Alderman, Sage and Chandler. However, the federal case against the National Workers League took precedence, they were told, though in late 1943, despite a federal grand jury in the District of Columbia indicting Alderman and Sage and a number of others for conspiring with German officials, the cases were ultimately dismissed. Federal prosecutors concluded that there were too many holes in the case to procure convictions against any of the alleged perpetrators of the various conspiracies. Likewise, the local cases were dismissed on similar grounds. After two years of motions and delays, Alderman, Sage and Chandler walked.[65]

Housing conditions during the war sharpened hostilities among Detroit's various factions, and the frustrations often boiled over in the war production plants. Throughout early 1943, a series of wildcat strikes erupted in protest over production quotas and hourly pay, which did not keep up with inflation. Occasionally, blacks walked off the job following disagreements with factory foremen and union representatives over job assignments and workplace discrimination. At Packard, personnel director C.E. Weiss, a noted racist who encouraged whites to complain to the union about having to work alongside African Americans, believed he could cripple the UAW from within by strategically placing blacks on the shop floor, where he knew confrontation might occur. On June 6, Packard promoted three black workers to the shop floor, where outside agitators, planted months before, could stir white workers, particularly Southern white workers who resented having to work shoulder to shoulder with African Americans. Twenty-five thousand white Packard employees walked off the job in protest. The UAW ordered its members back to work the next day, but thousands refused to return and picketed outside in the famous Packard Hate Strike. Under pressure from the UAW, the War Labor Board threatened to fire employees refusing to return to work. Thirty of the striking ringleaders were suspended on June 6, and the remaining workers returned to work.

Just two weeks later, racial tension in Detroit reached its apex following two earlier race riots in the United States, one in Beaumont, Texas, in which white shipyard workers attacked blacks following rumors of a black man raping a white woman, and the other in Harlem, New York, where blacks destroyed white property following a rumor that a black serviceman had been shot and killed by a white police officer.

THE 1943 RACE RIOT

Beginning on June 20, 1943, the costliest and deadliest race riot during World War II occurred on the downtown streets of Detroit. Purportedly, a racial conflict on Belle Isle, the nation's largest city-owned island park, escalated quickly and spread downtown. After federal troops were called in to restore order, the tally of death, injury and property destruction was staggering: 43 killed, 433 injured and millions of dollars in property damage, particularly in areas of black residential concentration. More than 1,800 individuals were arrested for looting and other infractions. Social psychologist Roger Brown, who was a high school student in Detroit at the time, recalled the buildup of tension preliminary to the outburst: African American resentment had deepened not only because of employment discrimination and the worsening wartime housing crisis but also because of particular segregation practices that arose during the war. The Red Cross, for example, barred black donors as early as December 1941 but relented later, reluctantly, by accepting—but segregating— African American blood donations. In the U.S. Navy, blacks were typically given the most menial jobs on board; the Marine Corps would not even accept African Americans. The indignities went on. There were strains for Detroit's white population as well, especially, as Brown recalled, because

> *they brought with them a set of ideas concerning the proper treatment of Negroes; ideas bred in a land of stunted opportunities where the Negro had been an economic competitor. These Southern whites were greatly irritated by the necessity of coming in close contact with the Negro at work, in vehicles of public transportation, and in public facilities of all kinds. Some of these Southern whites joined the Detroit police force.*[66]

The specific, immediate event that triggered the riot was lost in the fog of the evening's chaos, but witnesses suggest that a fight broke out between small groups of whites and blacks. The free-for-all spread to the MacArthur Bridge (or, more popularly, the Belle Isle Bridge), which connected the island to the city, and the violence spread into downtown. Fueling the conflict were unsubstantiated rumors circulating on both sides of Woodward Avenue. Two individuals told a crowd of black patrons at the Forest Social Club, at 700 Forest Avenue, that a mob of whites had thrown a black baby and its mother off the bridge. On the west side of Woodward Avenue, the white side, the riot was inflamed by a rumor that blacks had raped and murdered a white woman on the bridge. Roving black and white gangs perpetrated random acts of violence, such as pulling people from automobiles and streetcars; shooting or beating bystanders; looting shops, particularly along Hastings Street; and generally engaging in guerrilla warfare. Mercifully, there was little arson due to wartime gasoline rationing.

The riot was quelled after President Roosevelt sent six thousand federal troops to patrol Detroit's streets at the urgent request of Governor Harry Kelly and Mayor Jeffries. In the aftermath, Jeffries praised the police for exercising restraint, even though seventeen blacks (and no whites) were killed at the hands of white patrolmen. The NAACP's Thurgood Marshall later called the police commissioner's enforcement policies weak and uneven, as 85 percent of those arrested were black, and white atrocities were largely ignored.

Could one of the worst race riots in American history have been averted? In retrospect, all signs pointed to increased tension exacerbated by specific events such the construction of the Birwood Wall, the controversy and subsequent riot at Sojourner Truth Homes and the Packard Hate Strike just a few weeks before the June riot. Given the federal political realities

Cars burn near Stimpson Street during the 1943 race riot, June 21. *Walter P. Reuther Library, Archives of Labor and Urban Affairs, Wayne State University.*

of the era, desegregation was not a realistic option before or during the war. Significantly more public housing in general and defense housing in particular for African Americans might have mitigated some of the racial tension, but in reality, the major factions of Detroit, Polish Americans and Southern white migrants in particular, were largely implacable with respect to changing their attitudes and behavior at the major employment centers, on the streetcars, in the public parks and elsewhere.

Eventually, major changes would come. In one of the highly segregated enclaves of Detroit, the West Side, an important housing discrimination suit would eventually make its way to the Supreme Court in 1948 and produce an important civil rights victory for many newly protected groups.

As nearly every African American living on Detroit's West Side knew, crossing Tireman Avenue and journeying into the white section contained risks, no matter if it involved conducting business or simply paying respects at a funeral service. However, in 1944, Orsell McGhee took the unprecedented step of purchasing a home in just such a white neighborhood at 4626

Seebolt Street, one block north of Tireman. The seller, anxious to move to California, was willing to ignore the racially restrictive covenant attached to the property deed and sell the four-bedroom red brick house to a black family for $8,000. Benjamin Sipes, the next-door neighbor, filed a lawsuit in Wayne County Circuit Court arguing that the sale violated the deed restriction supported by the 1922 Supreme Court ruling declaring restrictive housing covenants lawful. Sipes's argument was upheld by both the circuit court and, upon appeal, by the Michigan Supreme Court. The *McGhee v. Sipes* case was combined with two similar cases involving racially restrictive covenants when it reached the U.S. Supreme Court. The lead case, *Shelley v. Kramer*, was set in St. Louis, Missouri, with almost identical circumstances. Famed civil rights attorney Thurgood Marshall, head of the NAACP Legal Defense Fund, would argue that court enforcement of such covenants violated the equal protection clause of the Fourteenth Amendment of the Constitution. On May 3, 1948, the court decided that though "there was no federal prohibition against including restrictive covenants in property deeds, no state or federal court could enforce them."

As important as this ruling was at the time—ruling racially restrictive covenants to be unenforceable—it would not be until the Fair Housing Act of 1968 (Title VIII of the Civil Rights Act of 1968) that significant inroads would be made in defeating the de facto power of neighborhood homeowners' associations, real estate brokers and agents and other nefarious organizations from exerting their influence to deter African Americans from establishing homesteads wherever they chose to do so. Ironically, after *Shelley v. Kramer* was concluded, Orsell McGhee and Benjamin Sipes became best of friends and remained so for the rest of their lives.

In order to counteract potential legal penalties, real estate agents and others who wished to exploit the fears and baser instincts of white clientele used increasingly subtle but no less effective marketing strategies in the years following *Shelley v. Kramer*. For example, in 1978, a real estate agent distributed the following flier to residents in the Wayne/Westland market area: "Just a note to let you know that we have new neighbors moving in. A new family has recently purchased a home, causing much real estate activity in our area. If I may assist you in any way, please give me a call."[67]

The implicit racial scare tactics would have most certainly been understood by white residents well conditioned by over a century of racial discrimination in housing, particularly in the highly segregated metropolitan Detroit real estate market. Almost immediately, most residents would look down the block to see if a black family had moved in.

Entrance to Sojourner Truth Homes, winter 2020. *Author's collection.*

Side entrance to Sojourner Truth Homes, winter 2020. *Author's collection.*

Two-story unit, Sojourner Truth Homes, winter 2020. *Author's collection.*

Today, organizations like the Fair Housing Center of Metropolitan Detroit field real estate purchase and apartment rental complaints, as well as complaints about other forms of housing discrimination in Wayne, Oakland and Macomb Counties. For example, people with disabilities were not a protected class under the original Fair Housing Act, despite the tremendous hardship placed on them by discriminatory housing practices. Unwilling to wait for fair housing law to catch up with the times, the Fair Housing Center initiated its first disability discrimination case under the Rehabilitation Act in 1987, one year before the Fair Housing Act was amended to cover disability.

In 2020, racially motivated housing discrimination is not so blatant as it was in the case of the Sojourner Truth Homes in 1942. But it continues to exist as property managers and real estate developers become more sophisticated with respect to their unlawful practices. Our growing understanding of people's needs—for example, as our knowledge of mental health evolves, we know that many individuals benefit from emotional support animals and deserve equal access to housing—suggests we still have a very long way to go.

NOTES

Introduction

1. *Detroit News*, April 29, 1942, 1, 2.
2. Carew, *Walter Reuther*, 34.
3. Peterson, *Planning the Home Front*, 183–86.
4. Welch, "Racially Restrictive Covenants," 130–42.
5. Ibid., 134.
6. Wilkinson, "Michigan's Segregated Past."
7. Lerman, "Substandard Housing," 41.
8. *Where We Live Matters to Our Health*, 2–6.
9. Rothstein, *Color of Law*, 21.
10. Washburn, *Pittsburgh Courier's Double V Campaign*.

Chapter 1

11. Anderson, *Education of Blacks*, 27.
12. Williams, *Detroit*.
13. Sugrue, *Origins of the Urban Crisis*, 36–37.
14. *History's Future in the North End*, 25–30.
15. *Remembering Detroit's Old Westside*, 85–104.
16. Dancy, *Sand Against the Wind*, 57.
17. Van Dusen, *Detroit's Birwood Wall*, 43–47.
18. Hopkins and Others, *Conant Gardens*, 51–54.

Chapter 2

19. Brown, *Social Psychology*, 730.
20. Capeci, *Race Relations in Wartime Detroit*, 67.
21. Levine, *Internal Combustion*, 71–72, 84.
22. Dancy, *Sand Against the Wind*, 133–34.
23. Kellogg African American Healthcare Project.
24. Moon, *Untold Tales, Unsung Heroes*, 313.
25. Ibid., 288–89.
26. Washington, *Negro in Detroit*, 180.
27. Dancy, *Sand Against the Wind*, 145.
28. Capeci, *Race Relations in Wartime Detroit*, 65–66.
29. "Frank Joyce."
30. Peterson, *Planning the Home Front*, 264.
31. Ibid., 266.
32. Dancy, *Sand Against the Wind*, 58.

Chapter 3

33. Rudolph G. Tenerowicz was a glad-handing political professional who understood that art of quid pro quo. "Doc" Tenerowicz, as he was known to his friends and supporters, graduated from Loyola Medical College in 1912 and practiced medicine in Chicago from 1912 to 1923. During World War I, he served as a first lieutenant in the U.S. Army Medical Corps. After moving to Hamtramck in 1923, he resumed his civilian medical practice. Five years later, with the encouragement of close associates, he entered the political arena and served as Hamtramck mayor from 1928 to 1932. In 1931, he was indicted along with twelve others—including two councilmen, the chief of police and a police captain—in a bribery conspiracy scheme involving transactions with the owner of a local blind pig and bordello. His popular support within the Polish American community never wavered, notwithstanding his conviction and incarceration in the Michigan State Prison in Jackson. During this period of Prohibition, Hamtramck was a wide-open town, and locals openly resented the state police entering the city to clean up "corruption" stemming from illegal stills and highly popular after-hour clubs. A petition drive garnering over forty-five thousand signatures had the effect of securing a full pardon from Governor William Comstock after Tenerowicz served eight months of a three-and-a-half-to-five-year

sentence. Tenerowicz received not only a hero's welcome upon his return to Hamtramck but also the keys to a new car handed him at a gala thrown in his honor. Doc Tenerowicz would go on to serve as mayor from 1936 to 1938 before accepting his party's nomination as a representative to the Seventy-Seventh Congress from 1939 to 1943. After the Sojourner Truth controversy, he would fail repeatedly in his bid to return to Congress, even after switching parties.

34. *Factual Expose of the Nevada-Fenelon Defense Housing Project Controversy*, 2.
35. Ibid.
36. Ibid., 3.
37. Long and Johnson, *People vs. Property*, 53.
38. Rothstein, *Color of Law*, 25.
39. Thomas and Bekkering, *Mapping Detroit*, 53.
40. *Factual Expose*, 4.
41. Ibid., 5.
42. Ibid.
43. Pehl, "'Apostles of Fascism,'" 463.
44. Rothstein, *Color of Law*, 26.
45. *Factual Expose*, 4.

Chapter 4

46. Black, *Casting Her Own Shadow*, 4.
47. *Detroit News*, March 8, 1942, 4.
48. Berman, *Metropolitan Jews*, 53–54; Bolkosky, *Harmony and Dissonance*, 236.
49. Buss, "Church and the City," 43.
50. Ottley, *New World A-Coming*, 254ff.
51. *Factual Expose*, 7.
52. Ibid., 9–10.

Chapter 5

53. *Detroit News*, February 3, 1942, 2.
54. Ibid., February 4, 1942, 4.
55. Ibid., February 10, 1942, 6.
56. *Factual Expose*, 7–9.
57. *Detroit Free Press*, March 1, 1942, 1ff.

58. *Detroit News*, March 1, 1942,1ff.
59. *Detroit News*, March 2, 1942, 1ff; *Detroit Free Press*, March 3, 1942, 1ff.
60. *Detroit Free Press*, March 7, 1942, 1.
61. *Detroit News*, March 8, 1942, 7.
62. *Detroit News*, March 2, 1942, 6.
63. *Detroit Free Press*, April 17, 1942, 6; *Detroit News*, April 18, 1942, 2ff.
64. *Detroit News*, April 29, 1942, 1ff; *Detroit Free Press*, April 30, 1942, 1ff.

Conclusion

65. Capeci, *Race Relations in Wartime Detroit*, 161.
66. Brown, *Social Psychology*, 721–22.
67. *Michigan Chronicle*, February 18, 1978, 9.

BIBLIOGRAPHY

Anderson, James D. *The Education of Blacks in the South, 1860–1935.* Chapel Hill: University of North Carolina, 1988.

Bailer, Lloyd. "The Negro Automobile Worker." *Journal of Political Economy* 51, no. 5 (October 1943): 421–29.

Berman, Lila Corwin. *Metropolitan Jews: Politics, Race, and Religion in Postwar Detroit.* Chicago: University of Chicago Press, 2015.

Black, Allida. *Casting Her Own Shadow: Eleanor Roosevelt and the Shaping of Postwar Liberalism.* New York: Columbia University Press, 1996.

Bolkosky, Sidney M. *Harmony and Dissonance: Voices of Jewish Identity in Detroit.* Detroit, MI: Wayne State University Press, 1991.

Brown, Roger. *Social Psychology.* New York: Free Press, 1968.

Buss, Lloyd D. "The Church and the City: Detroit's Open Housing Movement." PhD diss., University of Michigan, 2008.

Capeci, Dominic J., Jr. *Race Relations in Wartime Detroit: The Sojourner Truth Housing Controversy of 1942.* Philadelphia: Temple University Press, 1984.

Carew, Anthony. *Walter Reuther.* Manchester, UK: Manchester University Press, 1993.

Catholic Worker, March 1942.

"Conversation with Father Constantine Djuik [sic]." September 1943, Survey of Racial and Religious Conflict Forces in Detroit folder, box 71, Civil Rights Congress of Michigan Collection.

Dancy, John. *Sand Against the Wind: The Memoirs of John C. Dancy.* Detroit, MI: Wayne State University Press, 1966.

A Factual Expose of the Nevada-Fenelon Defense Housing Project Controversy. Speech of Hon. Rudolph G. Tenerowicz of Michigan in the House of Representatives, February 27, 1942. Washington, D.C.: GPO, 1942.

"Frank Joyce, October 17, 2016." Oral History, Detroit Historical Society.

History's Future in the North End. Ann Arbor: Taubman College of Architecture and Design, University of Michigan, 2013.

Hopkins, Clyde, and Others. *Conant Gardens: A Black Urban Community, 1925–1950.* Detroit, MI: Conant Gardeners, 2001.

Kellogg African American Healthcare Project, Bentley Historical Library, University of Michigan. www.med.umich.edu/haahc.

Lerman, Donald L. "Substandard Housing." *Rural Development Perspectives* 2, no. 3 (June 1986): 40–41.

Levine, David Allen. *Internal Combustion: The Races in Detroit, 1915–1926.* Westport, CT: Greenwood Press, 1976.

Long, Herman H., and Charles S. Johnson. *People vs. Property: Race Restrictive Covenants in Housing.* Nashville, TN: Fisk University Press, 1947.

Lutz, James D. *Lest We Forget, A Short History of Housing in the United States.* Berkeley, CA: Lawrence Berkeley National Laboratory, 2004.

Meier, August, and Elliot Rudwick. *Black Detroit and the Rise of the UAW.* Ann Arbor: University of Michigan Press, 1979.

Moon, Elaine Latzman. *Untold Tales, Unsung Heroes: An Oral History of Detroit's African American Community, 1918–1967.* Detroit, MI: Wayne State University Press, 1994.

Ottley, Roi. *New World A-Coming: Inside Black America.* New York: Arno Press, 1968.

Pehl, Matthew. "'Apostles of Fascism,' 'Communist Clergy' and the UAW: Political Ideology and Working Class Religion in Detroit, 1919–1945." *Journal of American History* 99, no. 2 (August 2012): 440–65.

Peterson, Sarah Jo. *Planning the Home Front: Building Bombers and Communities at Willow Run.* Chicago: University of Chicago Press, 2013.

Remembering Detroit's Old Westside, 1920–1950. Detroit, MI: Bookcrafters, 1997.

Rothstein, Richard. *The Color of Law.* New York: Liveright Publishing Company, 2017.

Sugrue, Thomas J. *The Origins of the Urban Crisis: Race and Inequality in Postwar Detroit.* Princeton, NJ: Princeton University Press, 1996.

Sullivan, Patricia. *Days of Hope: Race and Democracy in the New Deal Era.* Chapel Hill: University of North Carolina Press, 1996.

Thomas, June Manning, and Henco Bekkering. *Mapping Detroit: Land, Community, and Shaping a City.* Detroit, MI: Wayne State University, 2015.

Thomas, Richard W. *Life for Us Is What We Make It: Building Black Community in Detroit, 1915–1945*. Bloomington: Indiana University Press, 1992.

Van Dusen, Gerald. *Detroit's Birwood Wall: Hatred & Healing in the West Eight Mile Community*. Charleston, SC: The History Press, 2019.

Washburn, Patrick S. "The *Pittsburgh Courier*'s Double V Campaign in 1942." Presentation at the Annual Meeting of the Association for Education in Journalism. East Lansing, Michigan, Michigan State University, August 1981.

Washington, Forrester Blanchard. *The Negro in Detroit: A Survey of the Conditions of a Negro Group in a Northern Industrial Center During the War Prosperity Period*. Detroit, MI: Associated Charities of Detroit, 1920.

Welch, Nancy H. "Racially Restrictive Covenants: A Call to Action." *Agora Journal of Urban Planning and Design* (2018): 130–42.

Where We Live Matters to Our Health: The Links Between Housing and Health. Robert Wood Johnson Foundation. Issue Brief 2. September 2008.

Wilkinson, Mike. "Michigan's Segregated Past—and Present (Told in 9 Interactive Maps)." *Bridge*, August 8, 2017, www.bridgemi.com.

Williams, Jeremy. *Detroit: The Black Bottom Community*. Charleston, SC: Arcadia Publishing, 2009.

INDEX

INDEX

ABOUT THE AUTHOR

G erald Van Dusen is professor of English at Wayne County Community College District in Detroit, Michigan. He is author of *William Starbuck Mayo*, *The Virtual Campus*, *Digital Dilemma*, *Canton Township*, and *Detroit's Birwood Wall*. His scholarly interests include American literature and culture and local history, as well as digital technology applications in higher education. A recipient of numerous awards for innovations in teaching, learning and technology, as well as the 2020 Library of Michigan's Notable Book Award for *Detroit's Birwood Wall*, Van Dusen is a father of four and resides with Patricia, his wife of forty years, in Plymouth, Michigan.

www.ingramcontent.com/pod-product-compliance
Lightning Source LLC
Chambersburg PA
CBHW040407110426
42812CB00011B/2476